HOT COALS

A USER'S GUIDE
TO MASTERING
YOUR KAMADO GRILL

Jeroen Hazebroek and Leonard Elenbaas

STEWART, TABORI & CHANG
NEW YORK

CONTENTS

FOREWORD
WE ARE CHEFS

It's been eight (Jeroen) and five (Leonard) years since we first encountered the Big Green Egg and found out about the kamado. Both of us were immediately sold on this intriguing cooking device, and from then on we began using one practically every day. We still do.

Since that first introduction, we have fired up our kamados at remarkable locations: We've given demonstrations on both tropical beaches and alpine mountain summits. We've cooked in weather conditions varying from a freezing 3°F (-16°C) to a scorching 95°F (35°C); in heavy winds, rain, and snow, or while basking in radiant sunlight. We've cooked for world-famous chefs and shoppers at a local garden center, and catered to hundreds of guests with an exclusive dinner at our own restaurant.

Under all these different circumstances, while we often looked around in wonder, our kamados always stayed the same: reliable, responsive to temperature adjustments, and fuel efficient. We think now is the perfect moment for us to collect all our kamado experiences in a comprehensive book. Especially since these days, more and more people are discovering the kamado as an appliance that will change backyard grilling into full-fledged outdoor cooking.

Jeroen Hazebroek
Leonard Elenbaas

JEROEN HAZEBROEK (R)
AND LEONARD ELENBAAS

INTRODUCTION

Over the past few years, the popularity of the kamado cooker has grown rapidly. Each year, new brands appear on the market. Meanwhile, we have noticed an increasing demand from kamado users for information. The kamado has lured home cooks who never before would have considered firing up a grill in their backyards. After all, though this is an all-around cooking device, it is far removed from what we're used to in our kitchens. For many barbecue enthusiasts—and we consider ourselves part of this group—the kamado is the logical next step on the way to becoming better, more versatile outdoor cooks. It offers us more cooking options and more control over cooking temperatures.

Make no mistake: A kamado is no magic box. It doesn't turn you into a three-star chef overnight. Even in a kamado, the food doesn't cook itself. The kamado will, however, significantly improve the results of your labor compared to what you are used to achieving with a regular barbecue grill. All it takes is investing some hours in learning how to cook with this device. If you are used to working with a kettle grill, you'll likely have to unlearn a couple of things too. But with this book, we are going to help you improve your kamado cooking! To achieve this, we will discuss specific techniques and recipes for the kamado, and we will also take an in-depth look at the history and background of the kamado.

Brands and models in this book

In this book, we consciously don't advise what brand to buy. We understand that people weigh looks, cost, and quality before choosing a certain grill. For this book we have tested six different brands over a seven-month period. Each of these brands is used in the recipes and the cooking techniques discussed in this book. Considering the history of the kamado, which we will describe in the upcoming chapter, our selection of brands was quite straightforward. We worked with Kamado Joe, Grill Dome, Primo, Big Green Egg, Monolith, and the Broil King Keg. An important criterion in our selection of brands was their customer guarantee policy, because we believe that the level of warranty on ceramics is indicative of a manufacturer's confidence in its products. For each of the brands we used, we can offer good reasons to choose that one. In the end, however, they are all kamados.

Another thing we'd like to mention is that we have limited ourselves to working with standard models. Depending on the brand, they're called large, standard, or classic. These models have a cooking grid diameter of between 18 and 20 inches (45 and 50 cm). Almost all brands offer both smaller and larger models. The difference between these and the standard models lies mostly in their capacity. Only the smallest models, with a cooking grid diameter of less than 12 inches (30 cm), operate differently because some of them lack a heat shield.

How does this book work?

In most cookbooks, the reader will feel an understandable urge to immediately skip to the actual recipes, forgoing the explanatory text at the beginning. We put most recipes in the second half of the book; if you feel confident about your kamado skills and you want to start right away, by all means, go ahead! Maybe later on you can take some time to learn a little more about the background and history of this type of grill.

Our aim with writing *Hot Coals* was to answer the many questions we've been frequently asked during demonstrations, at fairs, on online forums, and on social media. We will address these questions one by one in Chapters 1 through 4:

· **What is a kamado and what are its origins?**
· **What are the inner workings of a kamado?**
· **Which type of fuel works best?**
· **What types of accessories are available, and which ones do you need?**
· **How does the use of a kamado influence the flavor of dishes?**
· **How do you fire up a kamado, and how do you control the temperature?**
· **What do you need to know about maintenance and repairs?**

There are a number of ways to use this book. If you prefer to first read up on the kamado, or if you're considering buying one (it's often quite an investment), then start with Chapter 1 and we'll lead you through the book from there. In Chapter 5, we grab the bull by the horns and lay out thirteen techniques, from grilling steak to baking pizza. Each technique is illustrated with a simple recipe—using as few ingredients as possible—that allows you to fully concentrate on mastering the technique itself. By combining these recipes, you can create a couple of menus. Finally, in Chapter 6, you will find nineteen recipes in which we go over all the discussed techniques once more. Some recipes are easy to prepare; others—the pig head rillettes, for instance, or the turkey—require more effort, time, and bravery. You will notice how, with this book in hand, you will be increasingly enticed to prepare your daily meal on the kamado. Not just meat and fish, but also vegetables, breads, and desserts; and not just during the summer, but throughout the year.

CHAPTER 1
THE HISTORY OF THE KAMADO

To better understand the configuration and workings of the kamado, it is important to take a closer look at its history. We weren't satisfied with the version of its history as told by many websites and manuals of modern kamado brands. These often consisted of a vague reference to a Chinese cooking device dating from the Qin dynasty, followed by a glowing story about the founder of the brand in question. We went on a quest, looking for kamado references in books on culinary history and cooking techniques. We also researched a score of obscure online sources, coming across interesting websites from both Japan and the United States.

FIRE PIT

A kamado is a ceramic barbecue grill and oven, which in its current iteration has been around for a little more than a century. If it weren't for the American military presence in Japan during the aftermath of World War II, we most likely would have never heard of kamados. The origins of ceramic vessels date back further, at least five thousand years, by way of China and India and all the way to the earliest tandoors that were used in the Indus Valley (present-day Syria and Iraq).

THE TANDOOR

The tandoor has been the favorite oven in large parts of Asia, where it has been used for centuries to bake flat bread and grill meat. Today this ceramic vessel can still be found in many different cultures as *tandyr*, *tannur*, or *tanur*. We believe—without having conclusive evidence—that the tandoor is the predecessor of the modern-day kamado.

Cooking fires

Anthropologists are still debating when humans first began using cooking fires. Their estimates vary from 1.8 million to 130,000 years ago. What we do know is that the first known archeological evidence of a fire pit and roasted meat dates from about 250,000 years ago. Around 40,000 years ago, fire had become the most efficient way of preparing food. To protect the fire from the wind, Neolithic man either dug a pit or built a ring of rocks around it—archeologists recognize these as some of the most common and iconic traces of early human settlements. In order to store heat from the fire, man covered the bottom of the pit with flat rocks. River clay, which has the favorable property of hardening when heated, was used as a fairly effective insulation material. When a fire pit is lined with clay instead of rocks and—to preserve even more heat—the opening on top is made narrower, the result will resemble a proto-tandoor that could also be used as an oven. The oblong, dome-like shape is much more fuel efficient because of the convection and reflection of heat. Once the wood fire stops burning, the hollow round shape enables you to cook using the glow from the cinders and ashes as well as the stored heat emitting from the ceramic walls.

The evolution from this clay-lined fire pit to a free-standing earthen vessel required significant technological progress, though. It wasn't until 170 centuries ago that people in China first learned how to make clay pots. For a long time, clay pots were made denser and waterproof by heating them next to an open fire while rotating. Later, the use of a brick kiln became common. In order to bake a heat-resistant pot, a closed kiln oven was needed—one that was larger than the tandoor "pot" itself.

River civilization

The oldest known tandoors were baked in large closed kilns around five thousand years ago. The necessary clay could most easily be found in a dried-up riverbed. It isn't surprising, therefore, that the oldest tandoors were found during excavations of the earliest river civilizations: along the Indus Valley and in Mesopotamia. Between 5,000 and 3,500 years ago, the Indus Valley civilization was at its cultural peak, and its influence stretched out over all subsequent cultures in Afghanistan, India, and Pakistan. Mesopotamia—from the Greek *mesos* and *potamos* ("between rivers")—was located in an area corresponding with modern-day Syria and Iraq.

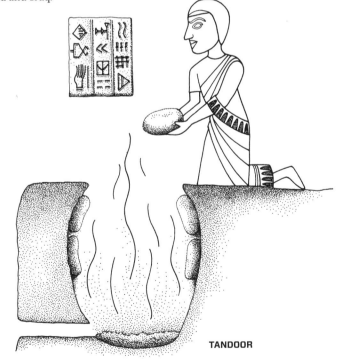

TANDOOR

The Mesopotamians were avid chroniclers. Their texts, written down in cuneiform script, functioned as handbooks for everyday life. From the harvesting of grain and the use of stones for grinding it into flour, to the baking of bread in a tandoor (*tinuru* in the Mesopotamian language, Akkadian), it was all laid out in great detail. Thanks to this civilization, we not only have the first written recipes but also the first complete cookbook. These contain recipes for Mesopotamian flat bread baked in a buried tandoor (with an air channel at the bottom in a stair-like setup, as seen in the illustration on page 9), as well as food prepared in smaller pots and dishes placed on the edge of the tandoor. This means the tandoor was used as both an oven and a stove. Because the Mesopotamians influenced other cultures throughout the Middle East, versions of the tandoor can be found from Israel to Azerbaijan.

The emergence of the tandoor and the oven goes hand in hand with the introduction of early types of bread. The tandoor is especially suited for baking flat breads, for which a thin slab of dough is stuck to the inside of the oven at a high temperature (around 750°F/400°C). The bread quickly bakes due to a combination of the tandoor wall's contact heat, the heat radiating from the glowing embers, and hot air convection. Today traditional flat breads like these, made with or without yeast, are common in many different cultures under names like *khubz*, *lavash*, *naan*, or *chapati*.

The form and function of the tandoor have remained more or less unchanged since classical antiquity. The area of distribution is surprisingly vast: throughout practically all of Asia, with the exception of China and Southeast Asia.

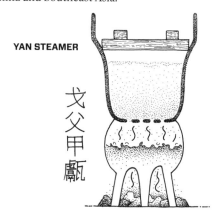

YAN STEAMER

CHINA AND JAPAN

As we mentioned previously, in parts of China the production of pottery began as early as 17,000 years ago. Unlike in Mesopotamia and around the Indus Valley, grain cultivation wasn't part of southern Chinese agriculture. Rice was the crop of choice. It was either boiled or steamed. The clay cooking vessels used did show resemblance to the tandoor, though, in the sense that the fire and ashes were confined in a round, hollow space in order to optimize the efficiency of heat radiation and convection. The Chinese name for such a fire chamber is *ding*. For cooking rice, a pot is placed on top (the *zeng*). During the Qin dynasty, another innovation was added to this process: In between the rice and the fire, a pot of water was placed, and the bottom of the rice vessel was perforated. The result is a Yan steamer, the first of its kind, which was created some 2,200 years ago.

Japan and the influence of the mainland

Like China, Japan never had a true bread culture. When it came to pottery, however, the Japanese were early adopters (12,000 years ago, during the Jomon period). During the Yayoi period (dating 300 BCE to 300 CE), the Japanese learned to grow rice. They cooked their rice in earthen pots over an open fire. During the Kofun period (250–538 CE), the Japanese adopted many customs and technologies from the mainland cultures of China and, to a lesser extent, Korea. Because of Chinese and Korean influences, the Japanese were able to improve their pottery. This ultimately led to the development of the first kamado, inspired by the Yan steamer.

The general meaning of the Japanese character for *kamado* is "fireplace," "oven," or "kitchen," a term comparable to our word "stove." The kamado was built into the house and often had a smoke channel leading outside through a wall. In early Japanese culture, the kamado formed the center of the kitchen, sometimes together with an open fire pit or a *shichirin*, a smaller fire tray made out of clay. It was used for cooking and grilling. Since the 1950s, Westerners have known this cooking device as a hibachi, which was seen as a more portable version of the kamado.

Sticky rice

Between the Kofun and Edo periods, the history of Japanese cuisine shows a shift from steamed rice to cooked sticky rice. The water pan was removed from in between the fire and the rice pot. From then on, rice was cooked in water in a thick pot or pan. The built-in kamado got its final shape during the Edo period, between 1603 and 1868.

Cooking rice on the original kamado wasn't that easy. First the pan (*kama*) had to be heated to bring the water and rice to a boil. Then the heat was tempered to allow all the rice to slowly tenderize without sticking to the bottom of the pot. This was easier said than done; this wasn't a gas flame that could easily be reduced. Moderating the fire was the responsibility of the eldest son's wife. She had the thankless task of having to reach through smoke and flames to shift or remove a block of firewood, if necessary. Once done, the rice was spooned into a wooden container. This stopped further cooking and allowed part of the liquid to drain. The choice of rice determined whether you had a dry grain or sticky rice; that is, if you had done everything right.

Recent history

The *mushikamado* (rice cooker) is the predecessor of our modern barbecue grill. They look almost the same; the only difference is their function. Somewhere during the development of the mushikamado, someone must have thought, "What if I put the *kama* with the rice inside a fire chamber? Would it be possible to retain the heat while extinguishing the fire?"

The practical solution was to place a *shichirin* (open grill) containing charcoal in a large tandoor-shaped pot. Thus it was possible to place the *kama* above the charcoal to bring the rice to a boil while letting air in. As the rice begins to cook, you close the chimney with a damper and the bottom vent with a stopper. The big difference from a tandoor is the outer shell, which is in two halves to allow easy access to the *shichirin* and the *kama* inside by lifting the dome or lid rather than working through the chimney. It's possible that this idea was sparked by Japan's introduction to Indian culture and to the tandoor in the nineteenth century.

Around 1900, the first round mushikamado with a lid was produced in Hekinan, a town on the Mikawa Bay in the southern part of the island Honshu. This area was known for its rich river clay and for the local production of *sanshu karawa* (durable ceramic roof tiles) and *shichirin*.

PROTO-KAMADO

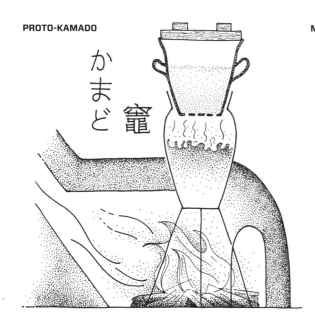

かまど竈

MUSHIKAMADO

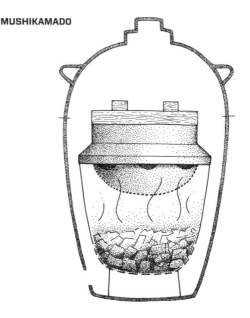

The fifties

After World War II, Japan was occupied by the U.S. Army. During that period, an unknown United States serviceman stationed there had the bright idea to use a kamado as a barbecue grill. We understand what sparked his experiment: Right after the war, Weber-Stephen and other American grill brands had developed the metal kettle grill. A kettle grill doesn't look that different from a mushikamado. Eventually, some of these servicemen brought mushikamados back to the States, along with kimonos and samurai swords.

Because American barbecue enthusiasts began using the mushikamado as a grill in the fifties, something remarkable happened: the development of a grill that not only could be used for gently cooking and steaming, but also had all the advantages and very few of the disadvantages of a tandoor. Like the tandoor, the kamado is suited for both baking bread and grilling meat, and there is convection, contact heat, and radiation. The fire box (*shichirin*) stands separated from the bottom, enabling the air to freely flow and the ashes to fall down through holes in a grid. This also makes it possible to adjust the temperature by regulating the airflow between the vent at the bottom and the chimney on top. The charcoal and the grill itself can be easily accessed because the lid can be removed—first by lifting it, then later opened using a hinge system.

Ultimately, the mushikamado didn't enjoy modern success as a rice cooker. The first electrical rice cooker introduced by Toshiba in 1956 became so popular that, ten years later, affordable rice cookers could be found in 88 percent of all Japanese households. Today you might occasionally spot a mushikamado in a sushi restaurant that favors tradition. They can still be bought for about the same price that a kamado grill costs in the West.

The sixties and seventies

The import and sales of the mushikamado used as a grill only really took off in the sixties, when two American airline pilots, Richard Johnson and Farhad Sazegar, began importing the kamados, each under his own brand name. Around 1965, both individually filed a patent application. Johnson bought kamados directly from a Japanese factory and then retrofitted them with

grill grates. He also added a sliding air vent to the chimney that could be easily closed and opened for heat regulation. The lid of the original kamado had handles for lifting it up; to make this easier, Johnson added a hinge. After these modifications, he resold the kamados to American soldiers for the affordable price of twelve dollars each.

Johnson is a controversial character to say the least. For more than thirty years, he's been accused of allegedly duping his customers and swindling his business partners. Still, he's also responsible for popularizing the name *kamado*. At the time, Kamado was the brand name of his grills. Sazegar, of Persian-American descent, sold his kamados under the brand name CasaQ (model Sultan and model Genie). His brand was moderately successful, and even published a kamado cookbook. Both brands were manufactured in traditional factories in Japan.

In 1973, a new kamado brand emerged in California. It was called Imperial Kamado and went on to become the new market leader. Today its grills are still considered to be the standard for kamados made from river clay. Imperial Kamado sourced its equipment from three small ceramics producers in Japan until 1995, when two of these manufacturers were forced to shut down. Subsequently, Imperial Kamado moved its production to China, which unintentionally led to the emergence of a completely new kamado industry.

Pinball machine

In 1974, the Pachinko Palace firm from San Mateo, California, began importing kamados. (A pachinko is an upright Japanese pinball machine.) At first Pachinko Palace bought its kamados through Imperial Kamado or directly from Japan, but later the company shifted to producers in Taiwan and China. Pachinko Palace came up with some imaginative brand names, such as Hibachi Pot, Barbecue Pot, and Sakura Kamado.

There was also another importer of Japanese pinball machines named Ed Fisher. By way of a side business, he began selling kamados that were often green colored. However, he realized that there were several issues with these clay kamados that prevented them from becoming a real success. Often, at temperatures above 390°F (200°C), cracks would appear in the ceramic material. The kamados were also heavy and

would regularly break during transport. They were good for slow-cooking and grilling, but the American consumer wanted to use them for more, like baking pizzas and grilling at extremely high temperatures. These demands called for innovation in the materials.

As it happened, NASA was doing research on heat-resistant ceramics around that time. As a result, the quality of ceramic engineering made great strides during the sixties and seventies. Through a friend who worked at Georgia Tech, Fisher got in touch with a brand-new, state-of-the-art ceramics factory in the Mexican town of Monterrey. This production plant had both the ovens and the know-how to make a kamado with these new technical ceramics.

Technical ceramics are a composite of several different materials (such as silicon-carbide) that, once baked, offer unique insulation qualities and durability. The coating was a challenge to create. Using materials like feldspar, a protective glaze was made that was capable of expanding and shrinking along with the ceramics without visible cracking. The Mexican plant created multiple test products and managed to combine the best qualities from each of these. The result was a more lightweight, durable, and heat-resistant kamado.

This led to the birth of the Big Green Egg. During the eighties, the Big Green Egg company, with its durable, heat-resistant ceramics, began taking over the market from brands like Imperial Kamado. This was the beginning of a following of consumers who became so dedicated to their green kamados that they called themselves "Eggheads."

Another American entrepreneur had reached the same conclusion about Japanese clay as Fisher. His name was Tarsem Kohli, and he was born in Punjab, India, near the origin of the tandoor. After returning to his home country to do research on heat-resistant ceramics, Kohli developed a completely different technical ceramic from the one that Fisher used; it was more porous and with a higher degree of insulation. The cooking results, however, were comparable. In 1989, the Grill Dome was taken into production in India. This brand solved the problem of cracking glaze by finishing the outer layer with several colors of heat-resistant lacquer.

In 1996, a third kamado brand appeared on the American market with lightweight technical ceramics. Primo was founded by the Greek-American entrepreneur George Samaras, who began producing a black kamado in Atlanta. At first his product resembled the Big Green Egg in both shape and finish. His most important innovation was the Primo Oval, a wide-bodied kamado that has a built-in system that enables users to divide the fire box and the grilling compartment into two halves. This allows for cooking both directly over the coals and indirectly above a heat shield at the same time.

EUROPE

European chefs quickly realized that cooking on a kamado is in many ways superior to other professional grilling techniques. Using star restaurants as a platform, they enticed their guests with the marvels

BIG GREEN EGG

GRILL DOME

PRIMO

of the kamado, and slowly but surely the Big Geen Egg brand began its conquest of Europe. The two other American brands, Grill Dome and Primo, soon followed suit, similarly first establishing themselves in the Netherlands and Belgium before entering the rest of the European market.

New brands

In 2003, Dennis Linkletter, an American entrepreneur and furniture designer, discovered a shut-down manufacturing plant of tiled kamados on the Indonesian island of Surabaya. Its Chinese owner had struck a business deal with Richard Johnson (the very same man who had started his kamado business in Japan in the sixties). It appeared that after delivering two shipping containers' worth of kamados, the Indonesian manufacturer had allegedly never received any money in return. Linkletter bought the factory and took it upon himself to completely redesign the kamado, using different materials such as refractory cement. He used new types of insulation and opted for a less-rounded shape. In this case, his decision to favor a front-to-back oval shape wasn't informed by capacity considerations but rather a way to achieve a different, more-even heat convection pattern.

This design led to the Komodo Kamado, the ne plus ultra of the kamado world. The Komodo Kamado cannot be moved without heavy machinery and the price is enough to give even the most enthusiastic kamado user pause. However, some of the most world-renowned grilling champions swear by it.

Since 2005, the market for kamados has grown strongly in both the United States and Europe. Thanks to the Pachinko Palace and Imperial Kamado, China had an infrastructure of experienced kamado manufacturers, but it lacked a consumer market. It was just a matter of time before someone would seize this opportunity. In 2005, the American brand Kamado Joe was founded there, followed in 2008 by the German Monolith. Both brands have their production in China's Yixing province.

In 2009, we first read about the Bubba Keg, a U.S.–made metal kamado—the first of its kind. In these grills, the heat is retained by a layer of insulation in between two metal walls. Soon after we discovered them, the production was taken over by the Canadian brand Broil King and the kamado was renamed Broil King Keg or Big Steel Keg.

Since 2010, large quantities of Chinese kamados have been imported to Europe and the United States under various brand names. We've heard reports about widely varying quality in this recent wave of kamados.

Over the last 120 years, the kamado has developed from a clay pot to cook rice into a versatile high-end cooking device built from high-tech materials. We are very curious to see which innovations will follow. What does the future of the kamado look like? What about the affordable Chinese version? Will design favor the easy-to-move metal grills, or the heavy tiled kamado? Or perhaps it will be a variation of some kind—a kamado built to each user's individual specifications, be they a cooking professional or a home cook.

KAMADO JOE

MONOLITH

BROIL KING KEG

CHAPTER 2
HOW DOES A KAMADO WORK?

RADIATION, CONTACT, AND CONVECTION

What makes a kamado so special in comparison with other grills? In the chapter on history, we talked about the origin of the kamado's shape and the choice of material. The kamado is (usually) ceramic, which has the properties of being a fairly good heat retainer while not conducting heat quickly, so the grill stores energy in the ceramic walls without losing too much to the outside. Because a kamado is an enclosed system with adjustable air inlets and outlets, the temperature can be precisely controlled. The heat source of a kamado is glowing charcoal. This charcoal heat is transmitted in three different ways: through radiation, contact, and convection.

Radiation and glow

A burning charcoal mass is hotter than its surroundings; therefore, it emits warmth. The source of this warmth is often visible in the form of a yellow, orange, or blue glow, though sometimes all you notice is heat on your skin. This radiated heat raises the temperature of the crust of bread or the skin on a cut of meat and causes them to brown (the Maillard reaction). Unlike microwave radiation, this heat radiation doesn't penetrate the core of a food product.

There are three things that will help you understand heat radiation:

- In an open fire, the efficiency of the heat radiation steeply declines when the distance increases. Twice the distance equals one-fourth of the radiation heat, for example, following the inverse square function. In a closed fire, like a kamado, the walls reflect back some of the spreading heat, but still the farther from the fire, the lower the heating rate. This means the distance between a hot spot and the cooking grid is essential.
- The intensity or focus of the heat radiation declines as the angle to the source decreases. A food product placed perpendicularly over a hot spot receives more heat than one placed at equal distance but under a sharper angle. This is something we can understand intuitively when we orient our face toward or away from the sun on a cold winter day.
- Radiation also has an indirect effect on cooking. The higher the temperature of the fire, the hotter the air between the heat source and the food product, and the more intense the convection will be. With more convection, more of the hot air surrounding the coals is carried to the cooking grate. This means that shutting the lid makes a positive difference when baking or grilling.

We refer to the radiation heat of charcoal as "glow" to clearly make the distinction between radiation heat from the ceramics.

Contact

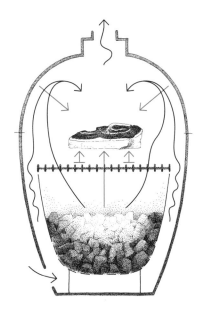

If a food product is in direct contact with a warmer metal grid or a ceramic baking sheet, we speak of contact or conduction heat. Ceramic is a poorer thermal conductor than most metals (which is why a coffee pot has a ceramic handle), and gives off heat more gradually than metal. For this reason, some people prefer to bake bread and pizza on a ceramic plate. The controlled release of heat causes the bottom of bread and pizza to brown without burning, giving bread its "floor" (crispy crust).

Metal is also denser than ceramic and therefore stores more energy in the same space. This high heat storage capacity and thermal conductivity are used when creating the beloved diamond-shaped grill marks. The surface of meat or fish in contact with the metal grid will brown quickly, because direct metal contact supplies more energy than the less-dense hot air between the grates. But cold meat will cool off the grill—so a thick, massive grate rather than a thin enamel grid produces the most dramatic grill marks. Cast-iron and thick steel grids are most effective for searing food.

Convection

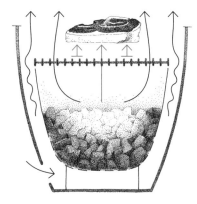

Convection refers to all heat transmission by the hot air itself. By partly blocking off the chimney and the bottom air vent, we prevent part of the hot air inside the kamado from escaping. This causes the hot air to circulate, whereby the round shape of the dome results in a highly specific flow. The convection picks up valuable flavor elements from the charcoal, like smoke, and deposits these on the surface of the ingredients. Moisture from the food evaporates and becomes steam, which by way of the convection is evenly distributed throughout the dome. Thus, convection heats up a product all around. The circulating hot air causes an even color and cooks the entire food product.

The illustration on page 17 will give you a better idea of how the three ways of heat transmission affect an ingredient.

Comparing cookers

Let's take grilling a steak as an example of different outcomes using different cookers. The main difference between an open fire and a kamado is that on an open fire, there is no radiation from a dome and hardly any convection. This has serious repercussions for the preparation of our steak (see illustration above).

On an open fire, there is a much bigger heat difference between the top and the bottom of the steak. As a result, the meat will cook less evenly. To get a nice result, you probably have to flip it more often. The immediate environment is also considerably drier, therefore more of the moisture in the steak is able to evaporate into the air surrounding the grill.

When cooking on a kettle grill with a lid, the circumstances are more or less comparable to that of a kamado, but there are differences. In a kamado, the fire box is a separate container, resting on the bottom of the grill. This gives it a second layer of insulation, so more heat is emitted toward the food. Apart from that, note that the single metal shell of a conventional barbecue grill offers significantly less insulation than a ceramic wall or a combination of two layers of metal with insulation in between. There is more heat loss to the surrounding air. Thus the grill will need to burn more fuel to sustain its cooking temperature, which in turn requires more oxygen. This will speed up the airflow inside. As a result, convection will subtract more of the moisture from the meat.

All of these properties influence the final result. More glow or contact, the level of heat reflection in the dome, the rate of airflow, and the control of humidity all factor in. Knowing these effects will give you a good idea of how we will apply them when discussing the basic techniques in Chapter 5.

Direct and indirect cooking

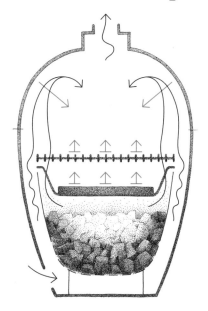

There are really only two ways you can configure your kamado: direct and indirect. Optional accessories like pizza stones, water pans, and cast-iron grids are meant for influencing either the heat distribution or heat transmission.

When grilling directly, there's no obstruction or shielding between the product and charcoal. The majority of the heat transmission comes from the charcoal glow and the contact heat from the grid. Convection plays a less important role here.

With indirect cooking techniques, we use a heat shield or a drip pan between the fire and the food. This prevents the product from receiving direct heat radiation from the charcoal, thus the heating of the product depends upon convection. A smaller portion of the heat is stored inside the ceramic vessel and will later be re-emitted by the kamado's dome (a metal kamado will transmit less stored thermal energy).

When baking bread or pizza, the contact heat from a baking stone is essential. Any stored heat in the dome also radiates and can be instrumental in forming a crispy crust.

KEY TO SYMBOLS

RADIATION	CONVECTION	CONTACT	STANDARD GRID
↑	↑	↑	++++++++++++++
CAST-IRON GRID	HEAT SHIELD	DRIP PAN	PIZZA STONE
•••••••••••••	⌣	⌴	▭

TOP, FROM LEFT TO RIGHT:
**CHARCOAL FROM ACACIA AND
AMERICAN OAK, AX, HANDSAW,
CHERRY WOOD BLOCK.**

BOTTOM, FROM LEFT TO RIGHT:
**CEDAR GRILLING PLANK, FIRE
STARTER WAX WOOD WOOL,
NATURAL KINDLING BLOCKS,
MAPLE CHIPS (LIGHT), WALNUT
CHIPS (DARK), HICKORY CHUNK
(LIGHT), WHISKEY OAK CHUNK
(BLACK), SAWDUST.**

KINDLING, CHARCOAL, AND SMOKING WOOD

Kindling

Everyone knows them—those white lighter cubes you can buy almost anywhere to start a charcoal fire. It's better not to use these in a kamado. They'll continue smoldering for a long time while spreading a nauseating smoke that will precipitate on the food. The same goes for newspapers, plastic, and cardboard. An inexpensive and useful alternative is brown fire starters made from sawdust, compressed with paraffin (candle wax). Most brands burn clean and produce little smoke. There are also oval bundles of paraffin-infused woodcurls available, which are about 4 inches (10 cm) in length. A third option is using a handful of dry wood chips. When using softer kinds of charcoal, a handful will suffice to get a red glow and, what's more, you'll immediately get a nice smoky aroma.

Charcoal

Charcoal is the product of pyrolysis, or charring. This process means the volatile elements in wood evaporate while the solid mass of the wood doesn't catch fire. What remains is a fairly pure carbon. The discovery of this process has been of great importance for not only the history of cooking and pottery, but also for metalworking. Some charcoal brands carry a logo from the Forest Stewardship Council (FSC). This indicates that the producer is using sustainable methods when felling and replanting trees used to produce charcoal.

Properties of charcoal

Our preferred fuel for the kamado is *lump charcoal*, in which you can still recognize the tree it was made from. The tree species used influences the quality of the charcoal. Hardwood produces a harder charcoal, which burns longer.

Every species of tree or bush gives a specific aroma to charcoal. This comes from the leftover wood chemicals that were not fully removed by pyrolysis. In general, the wood will not be completely charred; about 95 percent is carbon. Usually people pick a favorite type of charcoal for different reasons. The taste imparted by the charcoal works as a baseline on top of which all the other flavors operate. When choosing charcoal, burn time is less important than quality, by which we mean the size of the chunks and the amount of coal dust at the bottom of the bag. Coal dust is wasted money. We prefer fist-size pieces, because they will guarantee the best possible airflow control in your kamado. Since kamados are very fuel efficient, burn time is less relevant. Even when using the softest charcoal, a refill usually isn't necessary.

Types of charcoal

In general, European consumers have a choice between four types of charcoal, but choices for American consumers are even wider.

- **South American Quebracho**
  The name *quebracho* comes from *quebrar hacha*, meaning "axe-breaker." This charcoal has a high level of hardness and a high mass-to-volume ratio. The selection usually consists of very large chunks. Sometimes these are even too large for a kamado; in that case, we chop them into smaller pieces outside of the grill. Advantages are the long burn time and the relatively high level of pyrolysis, which means they give off little flavor. The bags tend to be rugged. Quebracho does have several disadvantages, however. Some brands tend to produce a lot of tarry smoke, or they crackle and spatter. It's harder for kindling to get quebracho to glow than it does with softer charcoal. Quebracho's dense texture also makes it more difficult to control the temperature. Another concern is sustainability; after all, this is tropical hardwood from South America.
- **African Acacia**
  Acacia is most often sold as professional charcoal. In general, the bags have an even selection of mostly fist-size chunks, which is an advantage when adjusting the airflow inside the kamado. The hardness lies somewhere in between South American and European wood species. The charcoal burns for a relatively long time and is easy to light. The aroma is pleasant. The sales pitch on the bag will inform you that this is deadwood from Southern Africa, but this is difficult to verify. One thing to look out for is the amount of rubble-like plastic, rope, or rocks at the bottom of the bag, especially near the end of the grilling season. This is a

result of producers being unable to meet the great demand for this type of charcoal. Despite these disadvantages, this is still our favorite charcoal.

- **North American Mesquite and Oak**
  Based on hardness, this product is in the same category as African charcoal, often containing a mixture of different sorts of wood. The selection varies widely from bag to bag, usually containing chunks smaller than fist size and some dust. The aroma can be pleasant, although some products use briefly charred hickory, which will cause a lot of smoke during the first thirty minutes of burning. Yet, for some kamado users, smoke flavor is all they want (see "Smoking wood"). Some brands carry the FSC logo.
- **European Beech and Birch**
  This charcoal is usually a mixture of beech and birch wood with a varying selection of sizes. Professional charcoal tends to have more fist-size chunks with little coal dust. The aroma is a bit drier and sharper than African charcoal. Since it's made from the softest wood of the four charcoal categories, it will not last very long. It is, on the other hand, easy to light and easy to handle. We have had several good experiences with European charcoal. Often, you'll find an FSC logo on the bag. Beech and birch are fast-growing species.

Why charcoal and not briquettes?

Briquettes can be made from many different sources: wood, for instance, or coconut shells. Just like when making lump charcoal, these sources are charred—but in this case, completely. What remains is close to 100 percent carbon. Subsequently, these chunks of carbon are ground. The carbon grounds are pressed together in a mold along with a binding agent, usually starch. Often briquettes have an extra ingredient added to help them sustain glow. This can be something like peat, sand, or even coal.

There are a couple of reasons why it's better to use charcoal than briquettes in a kamado:

- Because charcoal consists of close to 95 percent carbon, the remaining part being mostly wood gas, it burns nearly completely clean in a kamado. Only a very small amount of ash remains.
- Briquettes often contain an additive to make them glow longer, therefore they not only create more ash but also unwanted smoke and fumes.
- Lump charcoal in a kamado will burn hotter if you let in more oxygen and slower if you restrict the airflow. This makes the temperature adjustable.
- Briquettes glow evenly; they were made to burn that way. This means their temperature can be less precisely controlled. Once they glow, they will burn up completely.
- It's not necessary for all the charcoal to be smoldering in order to reach a certain temperature in a kamado. At lower temperatures, generally just 10 percent of the charcoal will be burning. The rest can be used next time.
- Even when they are made from natural material, as is the case with coconut or olive briquettes, they are not sustainably produced. It takes more energy to produce a briquette than the amount that will be released when you burn one.

The only type of briquettes we will sometimes deal with is the coconut. The best ones contain no filler and will therefore burn almost clean. Nonetheless, the only reason we would use coconut briquettes is if we couldn't get any charcoal.

Smoking wood

Charcoal is primarily a source of heat—for more smoke flavor, we often throw a few hunks of dry wood onto the coals. But which wood should you use?

It's not easy to describe the flavors and aromas of the various smoking wood types. Not just the tree species, but also the type of product (chunk, chips, dust) is important in producing smoke flavor. In the following overview we will take a well-known species and compare that to lesser-known ones. Within each category the species are interchangeable. We've listed them in order of preference.

Species of fruit trees

- **Cherrywood** is darker and sweeter than apple wood; it's a true smoking jack-of-all-trades. Excellent in combination with game and fowl, red meat, and spicy pork. We always bring along a block and some chips. Cherry will add a nice reddish brown color to your food.

- **Apple wood** is the lightest of all the smoking woods. Nowadays it's popular to add apple wood to soften the bitterness of the traditional oak. It works well with light-colored poultry and refined pork dishes. We always keep a stash in our kitchen so that we can throw it in the smoking wood mix. It adds a nice light brown color to smoked products.
- **Pear- and prunewood** tend to be a little sharper than apple wood and can therefore be used as good alternatives.
- **Grapewood** is still used a lot for grilling in France. These are the *sarments de vigne* ("trimmed vines") or *pieds de vigne* ("trunks"), which are comparable to chips and chunks. When used in a kamado, these pieces of wood will impart a sweet, mildly sharp aroma and flavor. They're a nice combination with duck, both wild and farmed, and a reasonable alternative for cherrywood.

Species of hardwood

- **Oak** is considered the standard for smoking wood by many people. We often compare the aroma of other wood species to that of oak wood. Oak produces a full, pleasantly bitter smoky flavor. It is suitable for any type of dish you can think of. If the wood has previously been used in a whiskey or wine barrel, smoking it adds an extra aroma to your dish (or at least to your smoking experience). Your food can receive a wonderful deep mahogany color from it. We burn dozens of pounds of oak per year.
- **Sugar maple** has a mild and sweet taste that fits naturally with all dishes made with maple syrup or maple sugar. It is perfect for salmon and other types of fatty fish, and pork with a sweet sauce. Maple is North American, but incomparable to American nut tree species because it has a much softer aroma.
- **Birch** and **alder** are less sweet than maple. These species are part of the same class; they share a light hardwood flavor not unlike oak. They are also perfect for salmon, but can be used more broadly with fish and meat products such as sausages.

Traditional American species

- **Hickory**, when used properly, is the king of all smoking wood. Where Europeans consider oak to be the touchstone for smoking wood, Americans rate everything against hickory. Beware, though: Too much hickory can easily render a dish bitter to the point of being unpalatable. It imparts a full-bodied, smoky, surprisingly spicy taste—like an extra twist of the pepper mill—to food. In traditional American barbecue dishes, it's often combined with sweet and sour, heavy sauce or glaze to mitigate the bitterness. Hickory can give your dish a dark brown color.
- **Walnut** resembles hickory, but is stronger.
- **Pecan** is a type of wood comparable to hickory in taste, but because it is milder, pecan is more forgiving in case of oversmoking.
- **Mesquite** has an intense flavor, tarry and earthy. This isn't nut wood, but rather related to the acacia. It is used as grilling wood or as source material for charcoal or briquettes. This is evidence that the source of your charcoal can have an influence on the taste of your dish, despite the fact that most of the tar flavor evaporates during pyrolysis.

Softer wood species

- **Beech** and **elm** are technically hardwood species (because they lose their foliage in the winter), but they are softer than the species mentioned previously. They aren't fully comparable, but are often used in combination with each other. In the Netherlands, our native country, these species are traditionally used when smoking sausages, certain types of bacon, eel, and other fish that are smoked on the bone. These wood types give off a mildly tarry smoke flavor, with a hint of bitter green leaves. In recent centuries, the preference has shifted toward oak and fruit trees. These days, beech will sometimes be mixed with oak to soften the smoke flavor.
- **Pinewood** smoking is mostly discouraged because of the resin, which can cause the food to get a tarry flavor—or more so than usual, as there always is a slight taste of tar or creosote to smoked food. In parts of Middle and Eastern Europe, on the other hand, people are very skilled at smoking on pinewood. A great example is German Black Forest ham. We have occasionally tasted some interesting results, such as pine needle–smoked mussels, but use of this wood usually doesn't go beyond an experiment here and there.

Sizes

Smoking wood is available in all sorts of sizes. We know from experience that the same amount of wood will burn faster if the pieces are smaller. Larger pieces tend to impart a less bitter aftertaste. Therefore, we always pick as big a piece as fits to the period of smoking, unless we want to smoke just briefly; then we always use chips.

- **Wood blocks**
  If you smoke food a lot, buying wood blocks gives you the best deal per pound. Because you don't need whole blocks in your kamado, you will have to saw or chop them into smaller pieces or chips.
- **Chunks**
  Chunks are pieces of wood of about 2 to 4 inches (5 to 10 cm) in size, ideal for smoking sessions of half an hour or longer. Often chunks will produce long-lasting smoke that isn't too intense.
- **Chips**
  For years, this was the most common and most readily available kamado fuel. They are easy to dose and perfect for short usage, for example when grilling fish fillets.
- **Pellets**
  This is pressed sawdust from a specific type of wood. It looks similar to rabbit food. We use it in the same way as chips, but it doesn't produce as much smoke as they do.
- **Sawdust**
  Sawdust directly on top of the charcoal is not suitable for hot smoking in a kamado, because it burns really fast and may smolder. To use it you need a special smoking box or a special perforated aluminum bag. We only use sawdust in a cold smoke generator (CSG).

Amount

Because a kamado is a closed system, it needs less smoking wood than other grills and smokers. We sometimes see people fill up their fire boxes with charcoal and then place a layer of smoking wood on top. That's overdoing it. Your dish will get an overly smoky and bitter taste. Instead, start trying out different smoking woods by just adding one single chunk or a handful of chips. Hickory is a lot more intense than sugar maple, so there is a bigger risk of using too much of it. Once you have tasted a dish, you can adjust the amount for your second attempt.

Soaking

Most types of wood don't need to be soaked. This is because they are being sold with a humidity level of 13 to 14 percent, which is traditionally considered to be perfect for smoking. Because of their density, the hardest hardwoods don't absorb much water. For bigger chunks, soaking makes little difference because the moisture needs days to penetrate more than a couple millimeters into the wood. If you happened to have bought a paper bag of wood chips that has been on display for months in a store window, soaking could be an option.

When using chips, however, soaking usually doesn't hurt. Watch out for mold and bacteria, especially when soaking for a longer period of time (several days). Adding a few drops of hard liquor to your soaking basin is a nice additive. We often use Calvados when soaking apple, Armagnac for cherry, and whiskey for oak. It is questionable whether dinner guests will be able to discern this aroma in their dish, but they will definitely smell it when they are gathered around the kamado. Grilling for guests always has an element of show cooking anyway, so a whiff of aroma to enhance the experience is never a bad idea.

Wooden grill planks

In the smoking section, we weren't very enthusiastic about the use of pine or cedar for smoking. When used as a grilling plank for cooking dishes at high temperatures for a short time, though, cedar actually is one of the most applied wood types, along with alder. Because planks are first soaked in water for a certain amount of time, their function is a bit different from the wood used during hot smoking. They are steaming as well as flavoring. Soft wood absorbs water more easily than hardwood. Hence, the preference for cedar and alder.

Also, the smell and flavor of smoking cedar turns out to be pleasant, making this wood an even better option for a grill plank.

FROM TOP TO BOTTOM AND
FROM LEFT TO RIGHT:
**ENAMEL GRILLING GRATE, STAINLESS
STEEL GRATE, CAST-IRON GRATE, HEAT
SHIELD, KAMADO JOE RACK, GRILL
DOME, PIZZA STONES (3), HEAT SHIELD
MONOLITH, CONVEGGTOR.**

HOW DOES A KAMADO WORK? CHAPTER 2

FROM TOP TO BOTTOM AND
FROM LEFT TO RIGHT:
**HALF-MOON CAST-IRON GRILLING GRIDDLE,
SKILLET, WOK TOPPER, STAINLESS STEEL
DRIP PAN, COPPER POT, ALUMINUM DRIP
PAN, RAISED GRATE, ENAMEL DRIP PAN,
DUTCH OVEN, GRILL WOK.**

ACCESSORIES

In this part of the book we will limit ourselves to the accessories that are essential for the techniques that will be discussed in Chapter 5.

- Heat shield and pizza stone
- Grilling grids
- Raised grids and specialty grids
- Grill plates, skillets, and Dutch ovens (we discuss the positioning for these in Chapter 5)

Heat shields and pizza stones

All of the brands of kamado we have worked with offer a ceramic (or metal) heat shield. Although each of these shields works a little bit differently, the general principle is the same.

- **Big Green Egg:** ConvEGGtor, formerly called plate setter. The heat shield is made from one piece; there are no loose racks necessary to raise the grate. The upper part of the fire box has notches that allow you to raise or lower the grate. For each model there is a matching ConvEGGtor. One downside of these ConvEGGtors is that their ceramic legs obstruct the airflow inside the Egg. The pizza stones come in three different sizes: 21 inches (53 cm) for the extra-large model only; 14 inches (36 cm) for the large; and 12 inches (30.5 cm) for the medium.
- **Primo:** The drip pan racks and the D-plates together form the heat shield. In a Primo Oval, everything works in two parts, which enables you to use the workspace for two separate food preparations simultaneously. The racks hang rather low and are meant to be used for both the drip pans and the D-plates. The rack can also be used as a deep grid for grilling at higher temperatures. The D-plates do leave about 1 inch (2 cm) of space to allow for air circulation. When you're using both D-plates, there will be a small gap in the middle through which hot air will flow. The pizza stone is actually the only round element in a Primo Oval. There is a large one of 16 inches (40 cm) for the Oval XL and the round Primo Kamado. Primo also offers a stone with a black porcelain glaze that should prevent sticking. The smaller 13-inch

(33-cm) unglazed stone fits the Oval Junior and the Oval Large.

- **Grill Dome:** The indirect cooking rack and the pizza stone together form the heat shield. The rack is meant for holding a drip pan or a ceramic stone. It hangs fairly low over the fire box, but compared to other brands it does leave more room around the stone for air circulation. As a bonus, this grid can also be used for high-temperature grilling by simply decreasing the distance between food and charcoal. So if the 13-inch (33-cm) pizza stone also functions as a heat shield, you will need two stones for baking a pizza (following the instructions in this book).
- **Kamado Joe:** Since 2014, this brand offers their Divide & Conquer system that gives you a functional two-way divide (like Primo) and has three tiers. Both the pizza stone and the heat shield, which is in two parts, have a 15-inch (38-cm) diameter. If you use both parts on the lowest tier, then the heat shield will shield off almost the entire fire box. There used to be a rack, as described under Monolith below, but with its own stones.
- **Monolith:** The distance piece is a rack that can hold two stones or a stone and a grid. The deflector stone has the shape of the Big Green Egg ConvEGG-tor, though without the legs. It can be positioned at the bottom of the rack. The pizza stone has a diameter of 14 inches (35 cm).
- **Broil King Keg:** The diffuser kit is a deep rack around the standard grid, made to fit a matching drip pan. As a useful detail: the Big Green Egg ConvEGGtor fits the Keg. Be careful not to damage the powder-coated Keg, though. The pizza stone has a 14-inch (35-cm) diameter.

Grilling grids: advantages and disadvantages

Broil King is the only brand whose kamado comes with a standard cast-iron grid. The other brands opt for either an enamel or a stainless-steel grate.

Cast-iron grids

Grids made from cast iron are ideal for grilling, but less useful for other cooking methods. Why this preference for cast iron, you ask? With properly seasoned cast iron, the grease that has adhered to the metal will prevent food from sticking. A cast-iron grid or skillet has a lot of mass, so it will transmit its heat directly but gradually onto the meat for better grill marks. This is different from wire enamel and stainless-steel grates; there, most browning has to come from convection heat and glow. The end product will therefore be less brown and sometimes even get the gray color of boiled meat. This is due to the lack of Maillard reaction. Also, cast iron is dark black, so it will absorb a lot more of the radiation glow than a shiny stainless-steel grid.

At temperatures above 500°F (250°C) for pizza and bread, you will burn off the grease-and-fat "seasoning" that gives a grid its nonstick properties. At lower temperatures, your food will often produce a lot of moisture, causing it to stick to the cooking surface. Cast-iron grids are also notoriously difficult to clean and may rust. Heat stress can cause a lesser-quality grid to crack. In that case, the iron probably contains air bubbles. And it's important to remember that cast iron is brittle, so if you drop it on the floor, it can break.

Enamel steel grids

For years, enamel steel grids have been the standard for all barbecue grills. They are simple to clean, don't stick easily, and are reasonably durable. After long and intensive use, the enamel may develop a rough texture. That's when it's time to replace your grid. A downside of thin enamel grids is that they aren't very well suited for grilling. The grids provide hardly any contact heat. A couple of brands have addressed this by offering you the option to use lowered heat shield racks as grids. At a low position, it is easier to catch a lot of the glow instead of just the contact heat.

Stainless-steel grids

Because enamel grids don't make nice grill marks, some brands offer a compromise: stainless-steel grids. These grids are easy to clean and also give your food that nice diamond-shaped grill pattern because steel is a better conductor of heat. A downside of stainless steel is that some cheaper grades of rolled steel have a tendency to bend back to their original shape after multiple heatings. This causes tension in the welding joints of the grid, which can lead to breaks. A second downside is the effect of salts and acids on steel at high temperatures. This will cause even the best-quality

stainless steel to eventually start corroding. The final disadvantage of stainless steel is that it will stick more easily than enamel. You need to oil your food before putting it on the grill. This will cause a greasy aroma that you may find unpleasant.

Ultimately, we believe that it's best to have two different grids for your grill: a cast-iron one for grilling and an enamel one for everything else.

Big Green Egg, Monolith, Kamado Joe, and Primo sell cast-iron grids. You can also buy a cast-iron grid from specialized brands.

Raised grids and specialty grids

Raised grids aren't just convenient for enlarging the capacity of your grill; they can also be used to increase the distance between charcoal and food, when you are grilling directly or indirectly, to regulate the airflow.

- **Big Green Egg:** The tiered rack/three-level cooking grid is perfect for building multiple adjustable levels in a large kamado. This way, you can increase the smoking capacity of your kamado from 6½-pound (3-kg) salmon fillets to about 15 pounds (7 to 8 kg). The XL comes with a simple but effective add-on grid that will double its indirect cooking capacity.
- **Primo:** For Ovals, everything comes in two halves. The raised grids are an integral part of the functioning of an Oval, because the brand prides itself on giving you the option to grill and cook indirectly at the same time.
- **Grill Dome:** There is an inverted raised grid, which has pretty much the same shape of the indirect cooking rack. It's mostly used for the pizza stone.
- **Kamado Joe:** The Divide & Conquer system has room for an extra grid level and half-moon accessories. There is a separate grid with three legs that fits on top of it for a third level.
- **Monolith:** The distance piece can be used to raise grids, both in the standard configuration and upside down. There is also a separate raised grid with three legs.
- **Broil King Keg:** Comes standard with a removable add-on grid that plugs into the cast-iron grate. It is highly functional, although it can be annoying to swivel it out of the way with each cooking action.

Perforated cooking grids and grill woks

When cooking small vegetables, mushrooms, and shellfish, we often reach for perforated enamel grids to prevent the pieces from falling into the charcoal. Various brands carry both a flat version and one with an upright edge (like a wok pan with holes in it) in their product line. During the summer, you will often be able to find these in the grill section of your local supermarket.

Grill plates and skillets

A grill plate should never cover too much of your grill surface; otherwise it will obstruct the airflow. Primo, Kamado Joe, and Big Green Egg sell several half-moon accessories that cover half the cooking area. We prefer to use a decent-size skillet. These cast-iron broiling pans with a short handle have the same function as a grill plate but can be moved more easily around the grill and are easily taken out with a glove. A skillet can also hold more liquids and gravy without dripping onto the charcoal. When you're done cooking, you can simply pour out the fat.

Dutch ovens and copper pots

The Dutch oven is the designated tool for stewing and boiling in a kamado. Using one turns a kamado into an even more well-rounded device, while at the same time magically turning the kamado back into the original mushikamado (see page 11). Dutch ovens are available in many different varieties and sizes. First you should check whether the Dutch oven fits your kamado. We prefer using cast-iron pots without legs, because the legs of a camp oven tend to get stuck in the grate, causing the pot to tilt. We use copper pots both with and without a lid to quickly heat water and sauces. Because copper is an excellent heat conductor, liquids will heat up fast. In cast-iron pots, the heating process is more gradual. Be careful with rapidly boiling liquids; a single splash of water on your charcoal can create a steam cloud that will dump gray ash all over your food. And, in some cases, the hot water may cause the ceramic of the grill to crack.

EVERYDAY TOOLS

Before you start cooking, lay out your favorite tools. This will help you mentally prepare yourself and avert the irritation of not being able to find something while cooking. For starters, you'll need a knife and a cutting board for your prep. Although a good sharp knife is essential, it doesn't mean it has to be expensive; what matters is that you can comfortably and safely work with it. As far as cutting boards go, we prefer wood or bamboo; those are better for your knife. However, a wooden cutting board, when used close to a grill, can easily get burn marks and blackened edges.

Next to the kamado we keep a pair of tongs, a spatula, a poker, a wire brush, a grid lifter, heat-protective gloves, a food thermometer, and paper towels.

You should lay out all the accessories you intend to use: heat shield, chicken stand, pizza stone, and drip pans. We use a lot of single-use aluminum drip pans.

Tongs

The perfect tongs are neither too big nor too small. Since tongs often are a cook's favorite tool for everyday tasks, preference is highly personal. In general, it's better to just spend a couple of dollars in a regular housewares store than to go to an expensive grill or kitchenware specialty shop. If your tongs bend when you use force, throw them out. There are a lot of inferior products on the market. A sliding ring to keep your tongs closed for storage is always nice. We prefer the standard restaurant-style tongs with their clam shell–shaped tips. This shape enables you to apply quite a bit of force, if needed, but also to gently lift up delicate fillets without a problem. Note: If you intend to use these tongs to move your grids and heat shield, they should be sturdy.

Spatulas and pizza peels

There is quite a bit of size difference between these two cooking tools. A flat metal spatula or pallet knife is great for lifting delicate meat cuts or fish off the grate. Smaller spatulas have a bent, offset handle, ensuring that your knuckles don't touch the hot grill; many people like working with larger spatulas about 20 inches (50 cm) long, because these perform all necessary tasks reasonably well.

On the other hand, a short-handled metal pizza peel works well for loaves of bread and whole pizzas, but also for larger meat cuts, bowls, and small pots.

In addition, there are many medium-size accessories that can more or less come in handy, depending on personal experience. It's up to you.

Do keep in mind that a wooden handle is more durable than plastic, which in our experience tends to deform easily. You've likely experienced it firsthand—you left a spatula on a hot surface for too long and saw the unfortunate results.

Pokers

A poker is basically a metal rod with a hook and with or without a grip. You use it whenever you need to move the charcoal in the fire box, whether it's cold or hot. It is important, for example, to stir the charcoal before lighting it, making sure any old ash falls down. Then, using the hook, you can pull the ash out from underneath the charcoal. This is why some brands call their poker an "ash tool," but it is in fact an all-around tool, which ideally should be strong enough to lift up a grid. Watch out with heavy cast-iron grids, though. They could cause your poker to bend.

Wire brushes

Because we usually grill with a cast-iron grate, we prefer wire brushes over brass brushes. A cast-iron grid is difficult to clean with a brass brush because the brush is too soft. Brass brushes also wear down faster. Steel wire brushes, on the other hand, can damage enamel- and chrome-coated parts.

The T-shaped brush is handy for a quick clean of your grid in between grilling. A downside is the risk of bending it when applying too much pressure. A thin and flat brush is great for cleaning the corners of your grid, or for scraping in between the rods.

Grid lifters

This is a handy tool for lifting grids, especially when they are hot. There are two kinds: the duckbill and the cross. We don't really have a preference. With the duckbill, it's best to use a poker or tongs to better distribute the weight. The cross tool is placed in the middle of the grid. You push the pin in between the rods, then twist the tool

90 degrees to make it grab on to the grid. Then you can lift the grid in one motion. In our experience, any brand will eventually bend if you use it for lifting heavy cast-iron grids. They will not last forever.

Protective gloves

There is no one set of gloves for every situation. You can have leather or insulated fabric ones for grabbing hot ceramics and grids; neoprene gloves for hot food, fresh off the grill. Leather gloves tend to get greasy and hard after several months of use. A recent innovation has been fabric gloves with silicone heat-protective patches. These work great at high temperatures and they can be easily cleaned by hand. Make sure to let them dry completely before reusing them!

Using dry gloves for wet tasks and vice versa can have dramatic consequences. Never grab something greasy or moist with a fabric glove and never use a plastic glove for grabbing metal or ceramics. For cutting and dividing food, tongs usually work just fine. When preparing large birds, disposable plastic gloves can come in handy. Sometimes a folded dishcloth is easier for picking up an accessory than a glove.

Food thermometers

For long preparations, we use an oven thermometer with a wire that leads along the felt gasket in between the dome and the base of the kamado. These are fairly inexpensive, which is nice, since there is a chance you will have to replace them often because their wires tend to burn out. When your dish is done, the thermometer will handily sound an alarm. For more direct temperature measuring, and when we have more than one food item on our kamado at a time, we like to use a fast-working digital food thermometer. By occasionally sticking its probe into one of your ingredients, you can keep an eye on the internal temperature of several dishes at once. The brands Thermapen and Maverick are popular, but there are other quality brands. Analog thermometers, especially the ones you can leave in the oven while cooking, are very imprecise.

If you want to automate control over the fire temperature, look at a PID controller like the BBQ Guru or Pit Viper. These have fans that you can hook up to the air vent to regulate the airflow, which is convenient when running the kamado overnight.

FROM TOP TO BOTTOM AND
FROM LEFT TO RIGHT:
SPATULA, FABRIC GLOVE, BURNER,
CHINESE TONGS, PIZZA PEELS (2),
DUCKBILL, GRID LIFTER, STEEL BRUSH,
KNIFE, THERMAPEN, DIGIQ, TALL BRUSH,
OVEN THERMOMETER, POKERS

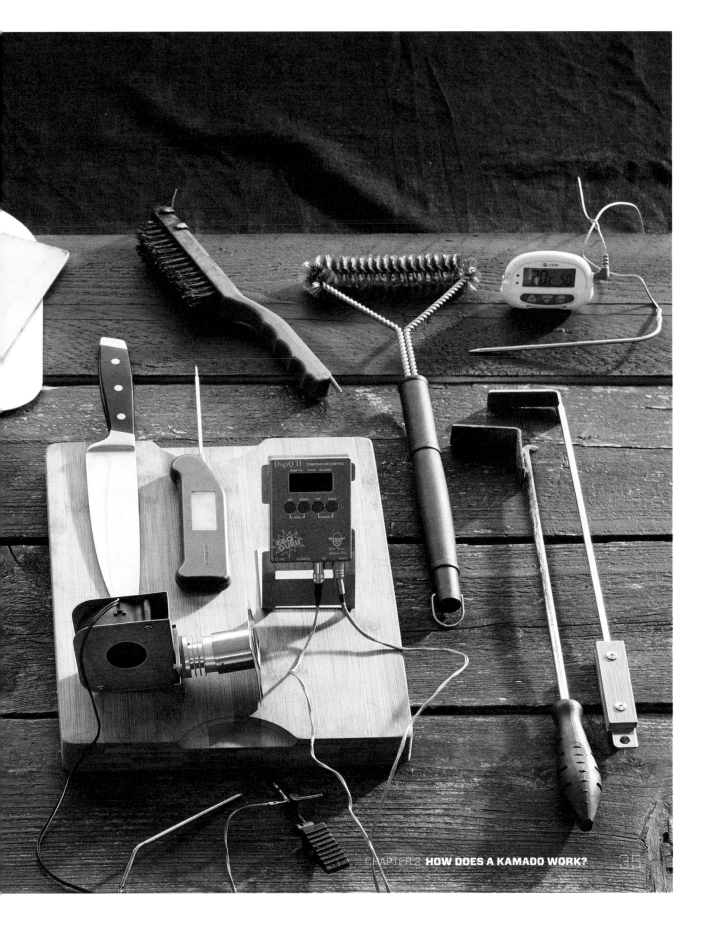

CHAPTER 3
COMPONENTS OF TASTE

In the previous chapter, we talked about the workings of a kamado and its accessories to give you a better understanding of grill accoutrements. At least equally important is to know how all of this affects the taste of food. How can you adjust the working of a kamado to influence the flavor of what you're cooking? It all begins with understanding what taste—in particular, grilling taste—actually is.

Let's start off with a couple of terms. People often remark how something has a smoky or smoked flavor when talking about grilled food. It's likely that they really mean the fatty fume-component of a food's flavor, but that doesn't sound as appealing, does it?

It's confusing. Smoke aroma comes from smoke, not from the grilling itself or from fried fat. Grill and barbecue flavors are mixtures of smoke aroma, browning reactions, and fat smolder. For grill flavor, browning and fat are the most important components, while the smoky flavor is subtle. For barbecue flavor, it's generally the other way around, because there's more smoking involved.

What is taste?

A brief refresher course about the basic principles of flavor: Flavor is a combination of tasting something with your tongue, tactile sensations in your mouth, and smell. Let's start with the basic tastes that we experience on the tongue: sweetness, saltiness, sourness, bitterness, and umami. That last one is complicated to explain; "hearty" and "flavor enhancing" come close. Apart from the basic tastes, we also sense iron, like in blood and red meat.

We can determine whether something is spicy, like a red pepper; it causes a burning sensation in the mouth. That spiciness is a tactile sensation, like greasiness, filminess, or crispiness. We are able to discern and describe all sorts of these sensations, from a tablespoon of sunflower oil to a dry biscuit.

The final flavor component is the aroma or smell. Our nose is a determining factor in how we taste something. Our language has many words to describe smells: rancid differs subtly from sour. Something can smell fruity, yet most people know the difference between apple and cherry aromas. Something can also smell greasy, buttery, or acidic. These sensations can enhance or offset the palate. In all of these flavor components, temperature plays an important role. The warmer a piece of meat, the more aromas it will release. (Animal fat is also easier to chew when it is warm, and chewability is a component of mouthfeel.) We haven't, by the way, forgotten the important visual aspect: "You eat with your eyes" is a truism if there ever was one.

How do we detect this in practice?

Meat lovers find the look of a nicely browned charcoal-grilled steak tasty. They imagine such a steak contains a whole lot of intense flavor. The crosshatched grill marks indicate that the steak has been in ample contact with the hot grid, which caused the browning. Based on the memory of previous meals, they expect a harmonious combination of sweetness, saltiness, bitterness, and a crispy crust. Perhaps the beef received a generous swirl of black pepper, giving it a nice spicy aftertaste. The core is medium-rare, with just enough chewiness to release the aromas and just warm enough to melt the fats. The result is a wonderful filmy core of meat and melted animal fat that gives off a slight taste of iron. The total complex of tastes is completed by aromas of caramel, ripe notes of meat, the smell of fried fat, and vanilla-like wood smoke.

This example shows how complicated a grill flavor can be. In the following paragraphs, we will take a more in-depth look at the chemical processes that determine taste. This chapter will provide you with the necessary knowledge to improve your mastery of flavors by making simple adjustments.

BROWNING REACTIONS: CARAMELIZATION AND MAILLARD

Browning reactions have the most impact on the appearance and taste of a dish.

Caramelization

Caramelization occurs when the sugars in food oxidize. This happens at temperatures between 212 and 395°F (100 and 200°C); above that temperature you risk burning the sugars. Caramelized food tastes sweet, but it does also have a bitter component. It has a specific smell that we simply call caramel aroma.

When grilling high-fructose vegetables or fruits or applying a barbecue sauce, a lot of caramel is released. When you are grilling meat, caramelization plays a less important role than the Maillard reaction.

Maillard reaction

The Maillard reaction is especially relevant when cooking meat or fish. It's a complex reaction in which sugars and proteins interact. Each time you cook food, hundreds of flavor components are released (like the organic compound furfural); together those components determine the taste and smell of the food. Although this mainly happens at temperatures above 315°F (155°C), it does occur at lower temperatures as well. The tastes that develop are sweetness, caramel, and bitterness. The mouthfeel is dry because of the crust produced by the higher heat. If you want to understand the influence of browning reactions, imagine the difference between fried and boiled meat, or raw pizza dough and a crispy brown crust.

Influencing the Maillard reaction

Depending on the situation, you can decide either to speed up or slow down the Maillard reaction.

- The easiest way to speed up the reaction, in order to promote browning and flavor, is by adding sugar and protein when you start cooking. You can, for instance, brush some egg yolk onto a sweet dough before placing it in the oven. You can also add a sweet rub to meat or fish you plan to grill.
- In an acidic environment (for example, when vinegar or lemon is in a marinade), the Maillard reaction is less successful. But an alkaline environment (like when baking powder is used in some types of bread and dessert) helps the reaction.
- Steam and moisture slow down the reaction, so in a dry environment the reaction works better. Using a drip pan with water during indirect cooking can delay browning reactions: During a long cooking process in a dry environment, meat can turn overly brown or even black, so using a water pan to add moisture can be a good idea.
- Salt extracts moisture from the surface of a cut of meat; it will therefore speed up the Maillard reaction when you are grilling and frying.

Burning fat and greasy fumes

Greasy fumes are a result of fat and juices dripping onto the hot embers. The liquids evaporate, while fats and proteins are only partially burned. This causes a greasy, damp smoke, or fume. The fats, amino acids, and other chemical components then precipitate on the surface of your food.

However, these fumes contain elements that are related to the Maillard reaction. The overall grill taste is actually affected by these fumes: They intensify flavors. Some aromas of smoke and the Maillard reaction don't dissolve in water but do dissolve in fats and alcohols. Because of the production and precipitation of alcohols like glycerol, produced during incomplete combustion of fat, you will get a sweet taste, while other flavors and smells will be enhanced as well. Burning of the animal proteins in meat juices leads to the forming of glutamates that also have a flavor-enhancing effect.

The tastes resulting from greasy fumes are bitterness, fat (filminess), mild sweetness, and a lot of umami. The aroma is a smell of burning, full-bodied meat, or bouillon (stock) and pleasant-to-slightly-rancid fat. Generally, aldehydes are seen as the most flavor-determining elements that form during the incomplete combustion of animal proteins produced by the meat juices that drip onto the charcoal. These are organic compounds with the aroma of fried fat and toasted chicken but also of burning and bitterness.

The question of grilling short or long

If you grill meat for too long, too much fat will drip onto the charcoal and your kamado will no longer be able to dispose of the greasy fume through the chimney. This is when unhealthy polycyclic aromatic hydrocarbons (PAHs) become relevant (see page 43). Sometimes we overgrill on purpose, like when cooking porchetta or picanha. By briefly grilling a cut of meat fat-side down, even allowing the meat to catch fire, we create a huge flavor explosion. You have to keep a close eye on the process, though; it can easily get out of hand. When that happens, you will smell a scent like candle wax coming from the chimney and the food can get a rancid or mothball-like aroma. It can even lead to dangerous flare-ups.

If you want to get a better understanding of the taste of greasy smolder, think about the difference between new and old deep-frying oil. When you are deep-frying, the same processes we discussed can boost all other flavors but also dominate them in an unpleasant manner.

Smoky aroma

Smoke consists of many chemical components, so it's not easy to accurately describe its taste and smell. These are processes related to greasy fumes and the Maillard reaction. When you're smoking meat, proteins and sugars from the wood are partially burned. The heady aroma of smoke that results is caused by hundreds of chemical components mostly in the phenol and carbonyl families. Besides guaiacol and syringol (the flavors of tar and roasting), the following chemical components are largely responsible for the aroma of smoke: furfural (nutty, roasted almonds), eugenol (clove, smell of spices), and vanilla (sweet).

The type of wood used (see Chapter 2) determines the ratio of these aroma elements. Many people describe smoke aroma as "bacon smell" or "roasting smell," but sticking your nose in a package of Lapsang Souchong tea might give you a good idea too.

How deep does smoke color and flavor penetrate?

When eating cold-smoked fish and smoked sausage, you can taste the smoke flavor all the way to the core. Until recently we were quite sure this is because of the low temperatures used for cold smoking (that is, if the smoke aroma hasn't just been injected into the food). You can also see this by looking at the color of the meat. Smoking has a preserving effect. Cold-smoked meat will change color all the way through. Hot-smoked meat only has a pink smoke ring along the edges. This discoloration is caused by an interaction between myoglobin in the meat and nitric oxide in the smoke. It produces nitrates that can slow down the growth of bacteria. This process can easily be replicated by adding nitrite salt to preserve meat, a practice often used by butchers when making sausage and pâté. It doesn't have any effect on the smoke flavor however.

An often-used rule of thumb says that the smoke aroma stops penetrating meat when the internal temperature rises above 100°F (40°C). At that temperature, proteins begin to coagulate. This principle is used for cold smoking, but we are gathering evidence that smoke flavor might work a little differently. The idea, for instance, that smoking above a certain meat temperature has no effect doesn't always hold up.

Like many other processes we have explored, things are more complicated than they appear. The fat marbling, texture, and moisture content of the meat are all relevant to smoke flavor. When slow-cooking on a kamado, at temperatures between 175 and 250°F (80 and 120°C), wood smoke can be added during the entire process. It is possible that due to hardening of the meat by denaturation and the forming of a crust at some point, the smoke no longer penetrates the food or only precipitates on the outside. Too much smoke can cause your food to start tasting bitter and dry. Our advice is to always smoke with moderation. Slowly increase the amount of smoking wood, learning through experience how to achieve the perfect result to serve your family and dinner guests.

If you work a lot with smoke and fire, you will build up a higher level of tolerance for the smoke aroma, though you'll still taste it if it is too bitter (something many American cooks like to mitigate by using large quantities of sweet rubs and sauces). Be aware: When you think something has a nice smoky flavor, your six-year-old might think it smells terribly burned and bitter.

TENDERIZING OR CUISSON (DONENESS)

Shoe leather or bloodred?

Tenderness is directly related to mouthfeel and texture. Often we talk about meat being tender (juicy) or tough (leathery). For the right balance, the proteins need to be coagulated just enough but not too much. The fats need to have melted and the whole has to be pleasantly hot, without being too hot to eat. The temperature, therefore, has a big impact on the doneness. This is why we use a meat thermometer. Imagine a steak that is well done and one that is bloodred. Many people favor one over the other, and that is perfectly fine. It's truly a matter of personal taste, but also of cultural background. In European and South American countries where the average local temperature is higher, we notice that people prefer their meat well done. In a hotter climate meat spoils faster, so it's safer to cook it longer.

FROM TOP TO BOTTOM:
RARE, MEDIUM, WELL DONE

How to measure doneness

Pressing down on a steak and comparing its firmness to your cheek or hand isn't much use when the cut of meat is thicker than 2 inches (5 cm). After cooking a steak for a while, its crust can be tough while the core may still be raw. There are external indicators for tenderness, but a meat thermometer offers certainty.

Fish

Because of the difference in texture, there are different rules for cooking fish and meat. The fat in fish meat is more evenly distributed. Fish also has a different muscle structure. Therefore, fish can be completely cooked at an internal temperature of 120°F (50°C), while beef would still be red or medium rare at that temperature. Generally, a whole fish will be completely cooked when you can easily pull out the dorsal fin with your fingers, or the muscles begin to flake. As soon as a white film of set protein appears on a fish fillet you are grilling, you can safely assume it's cooked.

There are fish with red or reddish colored meat, like tuna or sailfish. Due to a higher myoglobin content and denser muscle mass, they somewhat resemble red meat from land animals. The meat will therefore also cook more like red meat.

Crustaceans and shellfish

With crustaceans and shellfish, you can also assume they are fully cooked at 120°F (50°C), though many people will think it a waste to eat oysters completely cooked. The general preference is to leave the core ever-so-slightly raw to prevent the texture from becoming chewy. Flavors do intensify once temperatures rise above 85°F (30°C), particularly because you're forced to chew your seafood. Here the only advice we can give is: practice. Keep a close eye on the time to find the perfect doneness level for the food.

White meat

When cooking white meat like chicken or pork, we generally choose an internal temperature above 150°F (65°C), when the risk of bacterial infection decreases. For example, salmonella bacteria grow on the surface of a meat cut, and there are other types of bacteria that can penetrate the core of your meat. This doesn't necessarily mean that rosé (pink) poultry or pork is bad; it's just that many people seem to dislike raw or rare chicken or pork, as a kind of learned defense mechanism. In warmer climates, where bacterial growth is faster, it has always been safer to thoroughly cook meat. This shapes the general taste for the doneness of meat in these parts of the world. So there is no "perfectly cooked" piece of meat; it all depends on your background.

Point of Doneness and Internal Temperature

Rules of thumb

A few guidelines and a table of temperatures can be helpful:

- We aim for maximum flavor, which means that protein coagulation must have taken place. This process begins at an internal temperature of 108°F (42°C) and continues with a gradual breaking down of texture until the temperature reaches boiling point.
- The more fat a cut of meat contains, the longer we can cook it without it becoming dry.
- When we slow-cook something, a higher temperature than intended is okay. Proteins will have coagulated slowly enough for the meat to not dry out or lose its flavor quickly.
- Almost every type of fish is done when it reaches a temperature of around 120°F (50°C).
- There are almost no types of meat in which the taste will improve once the internal temperature rises above 175°F (80°C). This doesn't mean cooking it above that has no function, because:
- Generally, the connective tissues in meat need an extended cooking time at internal temperatures of 175°F (80°C) and above before dissolving into gelatin.
- Everything falls apart at around 212°F (100°C). Only certain types of beets and most potatoes are at their best at this temperature. The rest will become either soup, stock, or inedible.

Internal temperatures by approximation

Red meat
Beef, lamb, game, domestic duck breast

Bloody; Lukewarm	108–117°F	42–47°C
Rare	118–122°F	48–50°C
Medium-Rare	124–127°F	51–53°C
Medium	129–135°F	54–57°C
Medium-Well	136–144°F	58–62°C
Well Done	Above 145°F	Above 63°C
Stew	Above 185°F	Above 85°C

Pork

A Little Pink	145–153°F	63–67°C
Well Done	Above 153°F	Above 67°C
Pulled Pork, Spare Ribs	Above 185°F	Above 85°C

White birds
Turkey, chicken, most poultry

Done	Above 158°F	Above 70°C

Fish, shellfish, crustaceans

Raw, Lukewarm	86–104°F	30–40°C
Mildly Tender	104–113°F	40–45°C
Opaque	113–122°F	45–50°C
Well Done	Above 122°F	Above 50°C

Don't be alarmed if you find much higher temperatures online or in USDA sheets. We Europeans prefer to eat our steak a little redder than the rest of world. Often temperature tables are informed by health considerations, so before you know it they'll lead you safely north of the 158°F (70°C) mark.

PAHs and Two-Phase Grilling

This is probably the best time to talk about PAHs (polycyclic aromatic hydrocarbons). In this case, "aromatic" has nothing to do with smell. These compounds can likely cause cancer. Researchers often use the PAH compound Benzo(a)pyrene as an example because it's difficult to follow each of these compounds (there are many). These carbohydrates form during the incomplete combustion of organic matter like wood, charcoal, and fats. Incomplete combustion isn't just responsible for the forming of PAHs, however. It's also indispensable for grilling flavor. Any barbecue cook, therefore, has to take them into account. (By the way, during the burning of fats there are other harmful compounds being formed, but before we spoil your appetite completely . . .)

Scientific research

PAHs are organic compounds found in nature. They can be found in small amounts in vegetables, bread, and dairy products. For example, a relatively high level of naturally occurring Benzo(a)pyrene has been found in kale. One study looking at the presence of these hydrocarbons in our diets[1] showed the following conclusion: If you light up the grill once a week, the amount of Benzo(a)pyrene you take in will be less than 25 percent of your total weekly PAH consumption. Exactly how the researchers in this study were grilling isn't mentioned, but we assume they did not use the smart two-stage technique that we describe in this book. They most likely grilled using briquettes from beginning to end. It is therefore difficult to say how we should value this study in relation to our method of charcoal-fueled kamado cooking.

Various factors

In any case, grilling meat until it resembles shoe leather every day of the week isn't very healthy, but the rest of your lifestyle and eating habits play a role as well. Do you, for instance, eat enough fruit and vegetables? Do you go outside enough? Do you happen to live in a neighborhood where many diesel trucks are driving by? Do you smoke? (If you are a smoker, you can go ahead and disregard this section right now, as the amount of PAHs in cigarette smoke is many times the amount you consume when eating grilled food.) Nevertheless, we shouldn't underestimate the risks of grilling (or believe we should stop eating kale for that matter).

Reducing risks

According to scientific research, the most dangerous substances are found in steaks that have been cooked directly on a grill grid above the coals. Therefore, we want to avoid eating meat that is too dark. It also means that we want to make optimal use of the Maillard reaction, the burning of fat, and smoke formation to achieve maximum flavor with a minimum of unhealthy PAHs. We do this by cooking our dishes in two stages. One direct/hot stage and one indirect/less-hot stage (see pages 93–94). The second stage produces significantly fewer PAHs, so we want to extend it for as long as possible. As an added bonus, the core of your meat will cook gradually, resulting in a juicier cut.

[1] N. Kazerouni, R. Sinha, Che-Han Hsu, A. Greenberg, and N. Rothman, "Analysis of 200 food items for benzo[a]pyrene and estimation of its intake in an epidemiologic study," *Food and Chemical Toxicology* 39 (2001).

CHAPTER 4
USING THE KAMADO

Enough with the theory already. It's time to fire up your kamado! In this chapter, we will give you some pointers, but beware—even two models from the same brand can have subtle differences in use. You will have to get used to your own grill. Expect a half-dozen or more uses before you are comfortable with the kamado's own character. Only then will you get an idea of how best to work with it. In the meantime, we present you with an overview to get you started.

LOADING AND LIGHTING

1 Removing ash

Before you light your kamado, slide the bottom vent all the way open. Do the same with the chimney (with or without an adjustable opening). A good trick for never forgetting to open the bottom vent is to first remove the ash from the previous cooking session with the ash tool. Stir the ash to make it fall down to the bottom of the kamado. This also allows you to verify that the opening of the fire box is aligned with the vent to ensure maximum airflow.

2 Loading

We advise you to fill the kamado until there is 4 to 6 inches (10 to 15 cm) of space in between the charcoal and the heat shield—that is, if you use nice large chunks of charcoal. Depending on your kamado model, this means between two-thirds and three-quarters full. This is fuller than most manuals will suggest. It can be useful to mark the inside with a piece of chalk the first time around. Which brand you use doesn't matter in this case. Several brands provide better insulation (Grill Dome,

Broil King); we adjust for this by lowering the oxygen flow, but when you are loading the kamado it makes no difference. We have thoroughly tested this with six brands. We recommend loading like this for the following reasons:

- The mass of the charcoal slows down the airflow at low temperatures (175 to 250°F/80 to 120°C) when a smaller hot spot is used.
- We like to keep the distance between the charcoal and the grid as small as possible when grilling (see Chapter 2).
- There is no loss of charcoal as long as you reuse it, and you won't run out of charcoal when grilling longer or baking pizza.
- It's important to fill up the fire box until the charcoal is stacked higher than the holes in the fire box; otherwise the embers will receive oxygen from above, which will cause an irregular airflow and an unpredictable burning pattern.

3 Charcoal selection

You want predictable burning patterns so that you don't have to worry about your fire. To prevent unpleasant surprises like chemical smolder or excess smoke formation, it is a good idea to poke around the charcoal with your hands or your ash tool immediately after filling up the kamado. This way you can pick out any brown pieces (incompletely combusted wood) and pieces of string or plastic before firing up.

The airflow can be obstructed by ash from earlier sessions and small pieces of charcoal on the lower charcoal grid. This can make it very difficult to heat up the kamado to reach temperatures above 305°F (150°C). If this is the case, first empty the entire fire box. Select the best charcoal pieces from the ash and then add a normal amount of new charcoal.

We have discussed the choice of charcoal in detail. Still, it's good to know that even with the best brands there will be quite a bit of coal dust at the bottom of the bag. Once you reach the bottom of a bag, do not hold it upside down over the fire box. The dust and the smaller particles will obstruct the airflow during the first hour of burning. On top of that, you risk covering yourself and everything in the area in a layer of black dust. Instead, use a glove or tongs to grab out the best chunks and discard the rest along with the bag.

Lighting, step by step

We place the kindling on top of our charcoal. In general, we like to have glow in one or more hot spots in the charcoal. If, once the fire starters are burned out, we limit the airflow to a minimum (see pages 50–51), the glow will burn its way down to the bottom of the fire box. Fire burns toward where the most oxygen is, which in this case is toward the bottom vent. Alternatively you can allow more air in to create a more-spread-out fire.

Do not bury

Now, let's talk about a habit that might be hard to kick for many a pyromaniac: You shouldn't dig holes, bury the fire starters, or build charcoal pyramids. Burying your fire starter will not increase combustion. Burying blocks of paraffin can lead to an oxygen shortage and create smolder. The best thing to do is to put the cubes on top, in between the surrounding chunks of charcoal, giving them enough room to burn completely. You shouldn't place them on top of the largest chunks

because there will be too little contact between the charcoal and the fire starters. Create a visible hot spot. This way the heat can transfer to the grid more efficiently if necessary.

4 How many fire starters?

For slow-cooking or hot smoking, a single cube of starter should suffice. If we want to grill, we lay out no more than three of them on our charcoal in a triangular formation, about 8 inches (20 cm) apart (depending on the size of the object you're going to grill). When baking bread or pizza, we take two or three cubes and place them at the center. This will quickly create a high-temperature hot spot right underneath the heat shield.

5 Light 'em up

Use a long match or lighter to light the starters. We often use a little burner or crème brûlée blowtorch. While lighting, you want to see a yellow flame and as little smoke as possible. If the kindling goes out during the first ten minutes, it's best to just light it again. A small blowtorch is a handy tool for burning away the leftover kindling material. Smoldering and partially burned fire starters cause too much smoke, which will delay your lighting process. Wait until the kindling has burned completely. As soon as there is an orange-yellow glow in each spot where you placed a starter, you can start controlling the temperature—never before that moment.

6 Glow!

Glow is good. With a little more oxygen, that orange glow will soon turn into a blue flame while the core spreads wider. As soon as you have created the glow or hot spot you want, you can start tweaking the airflow with the bottom and top vents. Beware: Keep a close eye on your kamado while you're lighting it up. There are many examples of people who walked away, forgot that they were firing up their grill, and twenty minutes later returned to a kamado at 750°F (400°C). It sounds great when you plan on making pizza, but don't try to install the heat shield at that temperature. As long as the heat hasn't reached the dome, you can still get it under control. You can do this by closing all the vents as much as possible and leaving the kamado alone for twenty minutes (see "What is a back draft?" on page 53). The most radical way to regain control over a kamado is to turn it off and start over again. Sometimes this is preferable to hours of tinkering with a temperature that is too high.

Lid open or closed while firing up?

All vents should be wide open, but does this mean you leave the lid open as well? You can let the kindling burn with a closed lid under nearly all circumstances. This actually is one of the greatest benefits of the kamado and it allows you to fire it up during all seasons, rain or shine. This doesn't mean that the kindling will never go out, by the way. It can start to smolder because the air vent is partially closed, because you have buried it, or simply because you have bought inferior-quality lighter cubes. Of course, there are a few exceptions to the rule of always keeping the lid closed:

- If there is hardly any wind or rain and you have all the time in the world. It's nice to watch the flames.
- If you are protected by a roof or tent and you want to allow the smoke to dissipate as quickly as possible.
- If you are about to use an indirect technique and you want as little heat as possible in the dome during the first phase of the cooking process.

Other ways of lighting

There are at least two ways of lighting your kamado electrically: The first uses a heating element that you have to hold between the charcoal lumps. It creates a

broad glow within ten minutes. The second device discharges intensely hot air, which quickly lights a grilling fire. One spot at a time, you aim it at different sections of your charcoal, wherever needed. Of course we understand the appeal of devices like these. They work fast and cleanly.

ADJUSTING TEMPERATURE

7 Always closed

The secret to adjusting the temperature of a kamado is this: Give it less oxygen than the fuel requires for complete combustion.

That's why you are always squeezing the airflow or tempering, even when you are firing up the kamado or baking a pizza. With some practice, it's possible to adjust a kamado to within 5 degrees of the desired temperature. You can even achieve 2 degrees of accuracy, but that only works when using a digital thermometer. The standard analog thermometers in kamados have a margin of error of 3 to 5 degrees.

The closed system of the kamado limits the maximum airflow. Usually this is done by partially closing the sliding vent at the bottom and a pivoting round disk at the top. But even with both of these fully open, there's still the shape of the kamado as an obstruction of the airflow. Even though it seems as if a kamado burns hotter because of the chimney draft, it's a question of burning more efficiently. The draft helps concentrate the heat and store it in the ceramic wall, cast-iron grid, heat shield, or pizza stone.

What happens when the dome is left open?

When the dome is open, the kamado will lose a large part of its effective heat to the outside air. Now it is a regular open grill, without convection and glow emitted by the dome. The fire box can't be controlled. Because oxygen can reach the charcoal from above and from the sides, the flames will spread throughout the fire box. If you close it after leaving it open for a long time, all the charcoal will be lit and the internal temperature will rise very quickly. You are close to a back draft (see page 53).

Break the habit

It's important to swiftly close the lid after each action. Always shut the lid in a controlled motion. Never just let it slam shut by itself! In the long run, this could lead to the cracking and crumbling of the lid edge.

Every chef, especially the professional, has a tendency to contemplatively stare at the piece of meat they are cooking. For many, this is an important part of the pleasure of grilling. For kamado users who have other grilling experience, this is a hard habit to break (together with burying the fire starters). So once again: Turn over the meat and close the lid.

Air leakage

Air leakage is oxygen that unintentionally seeps in between the lid and the base. This happens when the lid isn't properly assembled or when the felt gasket has burned away. A sign your kamado is leaking at the gasket is the forming of dark stripes (*patina*) on the glaze around the hinge or the handle. Air leakage is especially bothersome when you are slow-cooking or cold smoking, making it hard to sustain the low temperatures. At high temperatures, it can become difficult to temper the kamado. Eventually it will cost you a lot of charcoal, because after you close the kamado, it will continue to burn much longer.

How to best align a lid depends on the brand. From experience we know that it's better not to just start fidgeting with your hinge; it sometimes even makes matters worse. Carefully read the assembly manual or contact the dealer. Replacing the felt is a relatively easy, but time-consuming, job. (See page 56, where we describe how to do it.)

Exceptions: When does the lid need to stay open?

Sometimes there is no other way. When you are cooking a large amount of smaller cuts of meat or fish, it's almost impossible to keep the lid shut. It takes minutes to flip every piece. In those cases, we try to work with roasting baskets or skewers holding multiple pieces at once. This can be difficult with fresh sausage links, which is why we prefer to roll them up and use a clamp. This is also why we prefer working with large cuts, cooked whole and then cut afterward.

8 Choose one position for the bottom vent . . .

Many factors determine how you control the temperature in a kamado. The most important is the relative position between the bottom vent, where the air comes in, and the chimney, where the adjustable vent limits the draft. Fortunately, we can give you a couple of guidelines for adjusting the bottom vent.

Some brands have a fine mesh behind the slide, preventing the hot ash from falling on your feet while you are cooking. This mesh influences the air circulation, so when using these brands (especially when you are used to grilling in your flip-flops), pay attention to this. If you aren't that experienced yet: Pick a position and stick with it. In this book we use pictograms for the three basic positions of the bottom vent. Of course, you are free to experiment all you want and to try all positions in between. The three positions are for:

Slow-cooking. The vent should be as far closed as possible without extinguishing the charcoal, generally at a crack about the width of a finger.

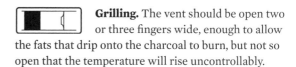

Grilling. The vent should be open two or three fingers wide, enough to allow the fats that drip onto the charcoal to burn, but not so open that the temperature will rise uncontrollably.

Baking bread and pizza. The vent should be nearly all the way, or all the way, open. For pizza, it's preferable to have a vent without mesh . . . and closed-toe shoes on your feet.

9 . . . and then adjust the top vent

Each brand has a different-model top vent. There are built-in pivoting disks that can be found in most metal kamados, and online you can buy all sorts of interesting third-party stainless-steel variations. The most common "daisy wheel" model has a double adjustable system: You can pivot the entire vent away and also adjust the size of the holes in the lid by rotating it.

This adds a little subtlety to the airflow regulation. In fact, the shape of the top vent doesn't matter much. What matters is that you adjust the temperature by opening or closing it. Note that unless you want to extinguish the kamado, never completely close the

vent while you are cooking. If you want to work at a low temperature (at 175°F/80°C for instance), then experiment with your own kamado and try to find the position where the vent opening is as small as possible without putting out your fire. When baking pizza, the vent has to be open all the way. In some cases, we even remove the entire vent.

An explanation of the icons we are using:

As far closed as possible. Barely open. Daisy wheel models are closed with the inlet holes at the smallest position. This position is used for cooking below 212°F (100°C) and for reducing the kamado's temperature.

Three-quarters closed, or open holes with a daisy wheel. This position is for cooking at constant temperatures between 245 and 390°F (120 and 200°C) and for gradually lowering the temperature toward 390°F (200°C).

Half open. Daisy wheels are one-quarter open or the holes all the way open. This position is for grilling and oven cooking with temperatures higher than 390°F (200°C) and for raising the temperature in a controlled fashion.

Completely open. Daisy wheels or holes are completely open. This position is for baking pizza or when quickly stoking up the kamado.

10   **Tip: On models with rotatable vents, we always make sure that both bolts on the vent are aligned** with both the handle and the hinge. This way the disk can't accidentally fall open, or shut when the dome is lifted.

A gentle way of regulating

Always make small adjustments when regulating airflow. Don't change the vent from all the way open to completely shut, or vice versa. Otherwise, you won't have much control over the airflow, and the temperature of your kamado can radically swing one way, especially upward.

Allow the grill about 5 minutes to reach the right temperature after every adjustment. Well-insulated grills can take time to reach the desired temperature. Once the 570°F (300°C) point has been reached and the dome has absorbed this heat, it will be difficult to get it back below 300°F (150°C), taking more than an hour. Sometimes it's better to extinguish the fire and start over from scratch half an hour or so later.

As we mentioned before, leaving the kamado open is counterproductive. In practice, it is easier to start at

a low temperature and to build up the heat from there (this is an argument for the "end sear." See page 94.)

When preparing a menu, keep in mind that it is easier to first smoke a dish and then grill something. Grill management like this will become easier with experience. After a while you will also become confident enough to step away from the kamado without worrying about changes in temperature.

It isn't forbidden to change both bottom and top vents at the same time. However, we think it's easier to first learn how your kamado reacts when you do everything with the top vent and leave the bottom one alone. There is another reason for this: If you find the temperature is too high and you shut both vents at once, you risk creating a back draft (see page 53).

Using the heat shield, drip pans, and raised grids

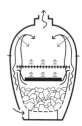

The heat shield is the most important loose part of the kamado. If it weren't for this accessory, you would have basically bought a very expensive barbecue grill. By installing the heat shield in the lowest position, you turn all of the space inside your kamado above the shield into an oven. That way the temperature in between the ceramic layers can be controlled from 160 to 525°F (70 to 275°C). For the higher temperatures needed for pizza, we use a different configuration.

Inside ceramic kamados, the food is surrounded on all sides by the heat radiation emitted by the ceramics. The convection will produce a distinct airflow that first takes the hot air up toward the dome, where it will curl downward directly underneath the chimney.

The heat shield and pizza stone significantly affect the temperature of the kamado. The temperature underneath the dome goes down by about 90°F (50 to 60°C) when you place the heat shield. There are two reasons for this:

- The heat shield blocks the direct heat from the embers, storing it inside its own ceramic mass.
- By placing a large obstruction to the airflow, and leaving the bottom and top vents unchanged, you ensure that the charcoal will receive less oxygen and burn at a lower temperature.

The heat shield is a pleasantly predictable instrument for regulating the kamado's temperature. (In case of the Primo Oval, we mean the two D-plates when referring to the heat shield.)

If we add a second pizza stone at the second tier, it  will initially reduce the dome temperature by another 55°F (30°C). This is not constant; the temperature above the pizza stone will level out. When working with high temperatures this can get complicated because a lot of heat will already have been stored in the dome. When making bread or pizza, we recommend you stoke up the kamado to the desired temperature with the whole configuration in place.

11 Drip pans, sand, salt, and water

When cooking meat or fish, it is always handy to place a drip pan underneath the grid, on top of the heat shield. The pan will catch any leaking fat and juices, making sure the heat shield stays clean. A greasy and dirty ceramic shield can lead to unintentional smoke and even cause a flare-up (see page 54).

If we fill the drip pan with water, we alter the temperature and the humidity in the dome. Although at first the temperature will go down, the higher humidity will actually increase the heat transmission to the food. Once all the water has evaporated from the pan, the air surrounding the food will become drier, the Maillard reaction will intensify, and more crust will start to form.

If you want low humidity under the dome, it's a good idea to fill up the drip pan with a layer of clean sand or salt. This layer will absorb all the fats and proteins. The pan will be easy to empty out and to clean as well. This trick works well for retaining that nice, dry crust after an initial sear (see page 93) with a minimum of smolder.

Some brands have drip pans that are larger than the heat shield. This size difference does affect the heat build-up in the dome. Sometimes using a bigger pan can help prevent the edges of a large cut of meat or bird from burning, because the hot air is forced to take a wider route around the meat. This lets us use the temperature disparity in the dome to our advantage.

Raised grids

Increasing capacity isn't the only function of raised

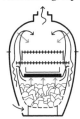

grids or grid extenders. They also can be used to smoke or grill at differing temperatures within the kamado. When placed on the second tier directly above the drip pan, an extension grid can be colder than higher up in the dome near the thermometer. This means the bottom of your food will be relatively cold. At the same time, hot air is circling down at your food from the chimney. We fix this imbalance by raising the grid so the food sits at the center of the dome. This has several advantages:

- The thermometer gauge is at the same height as the food.
- The convection ensures that the entire surface of the food gets into contact with the hot air, steam, and smoke.

12 Crackle and flame: back draft and flare-ups

Without giving it much thought, you throw open your kamado lid and all of a sudden you hear a crackling sound coming from the hairs on your arm or, even worse, your eyebrows, eyelashes, and hair. An unpleasant smell enters your nostrils while your guests are gaping at you in disbelief. You have just had your first experience with back draft.

Even we, seasoned kamado professionals, are taken by surprise by these flare-ups several times a year (including the unintended hair loss). So there is no need to feel ashamed when it first happens to you. Although these back drafts aren't completely harmless, they are mostly just inconvenient—especially if you value your facial hair. Usually the worst that can happen is a first-degree (the lightest grade) burn on your hands or arms.

What is a back draft?

Back draft happens when you initially burn your fuel (charcoal) too hot. This could be caused by leaving the lid open for too long, or by having the vent completely open. If you subsequently close the lid or squeeze the

air supply by reducing the vent opening, the charcoal will hanker for oxygen. It will burn up all available oxygen inside the kamado, start to cool off, and create a vacuum. This will last several minutes until the charcoal extinguishes partly, causing the kamado to repressurize. If you open the lid too quickly, you will notice air is being sucked in through the opening. Lifting the lid allows a burst of incoming air to give the charcoal a fresh supply of oxygen that will suddenly make it burn more intensely, causing hot blue flames. The air then expands and wants to escape, blowing the blue flames in your direction. You are standing in front of the opening after all . . .

How to prevent a back draft

First make sure that you have full control over the kamado; don't just allow the temperature to go up to 570 to 750°F (300 to 400°C) without a heat shield in place. When your kamado is really hot, never leave the lid open for more than a minute. If you notice that the charcoal is glowing a dark orange, close the lid and step away for at least five minutes. Don't try to immediately reduce the openings as far as possible. It's better to do this after the low pressure has waned.

If you have to access the grid because you need to take something off, first lift the lid no more than about 4 inches (10 cm). This is called "burping."

If, while doing this, a blue flame bursts from the crack, you will probably only lose some hairs on your knuckles and the back of your hand. This is where a fireproof glove can come in handy. Next, open the dome with caution and quickly remove the food from the grid. Close the lid and leave the kamado for about five minutes.

With a heat shield, back drafts do occur occasionally, but the blue flame will be less intense because the shield will block most of the air circulation.

What is a flare-up?

A flare-up resembles a back draft, in the sense that there is insufficient oxygen for burning all the fuel. Flare-ups can be a little more dangerous but in general are manageable. A flare-up is the result of not just the oxygen-starved charcoal but also the fat dripping from a piece of meat or fish getting insufficient oxygen. You can predict a flare-up when heavy smoke with the smell of candle wax is billowing from the chimney. This indicates that the incomplete combustion of fats is taking place. Then these burned fats hover inside the dome in the form of greasy smoke (containing unhealthy PAHs). Now you have to be careful. If you open the lid, the fat will ignite, but since there isn't heavy pressure, the flame will be yellow instead of blue. This can burn longer than a blue back draft.

A flare-up usually occurs while you are grilling, often when you are about to turn over the meat. If you have only one piece of meat, it will be just one yellow flame right below the food, but if you have a grill full of meat, there is a risk of your whole fire box turning into one large sea of flames. In that scenario, all the fats dripping onto the charcoal catch fire at once.

Flare-ups can also come from the heat shield. In that case, the fat has been absorbed by the ceramics. Once the ceramic gets sufficiently hot, the fat will start burning and flaming (usually not too intensely). This is mostly irritating because it can take a while before the stone has burned off all the fat. You can prevent these flare-ups by using a drip pan.

When the chimney is billowing smoke

To stop a flare-up, grab a fireproof glove or mitt and the longest barbecue tongs you have. Open the lid at a crack of about 4 inches (10 cm) and burp the kamado. Don't hover over the opening. This is when flames can burst out from under the dome. Hold the lid in this position for a couple of seconds in order to let the greasy fumes escape. Now slowly open the lid and take a step back to assess the situation.

A couple of flames right underneath your food won't do much harm; they will go out once you close the lid. Simply move the pieces you want to grill to another section of the grid and continue cooking. If all the charcoal is flaming up, there is no other option than temporarily clearing the grid. Transfer the food to a platter until the kamado has burned away most of the drippings. The best thing to do now is to put both bottom and top vents in the half-open position to allow the smolder to escape. Otherwise, it can take a long time before your kamado is back to normal.

Once the smoke from the chimney has decreased (after about ten minutes), you can bring the kamado to the desired temperature again. Don't close off everything at once, though, since during the burning of the fats the temperature may have gone up considerably. If you subsequently open the lid, you run the risk of a back draft, which would be going full circle.

SHUTTING DOWN, STORAGE, AND MAINTENANCE

Shutting down

After you are finished cooking, close both the bottom and top vents all the way. Only Grill Dome kamados have a warranty condition stating that the dome temperature needs to be below 300°F (150°C) before you close off everything. If the felt gasket is in good condition and there is no false air being sucked in, the kamado will go out within fifteen minutes. The speed at which the kamado cools down depends on the insulation and the material it's made of, but expect it to take at least an hour.

The leftover charcoal can be used next time. Note that if you never completely burn up all the charcoal, the leftover pieces will get ever smaller. After five sessions, there will be pieces the size of pebbles lying at the bottom. These will obstruct the air circulation to the point where it can become difficult to really stoke the kamado up to high temperatures.

It's possible to empty the fire box after using the kamado five times (once it's completely cooled down) and to discard all unusable charcoal. It's even better to burn up everything once in a while with a high-heat burn-off. This will also burn away old food smells and leftover fats.

Storage and covers

Most kamados can be left outside year-round without a problem. Some parts, however, do rust. Therefore it's recommended that you store your kamado under a roof or inside a shed when not using it for a longer period of time. If you don't have indoor storage, use a cover.

Underneath covers without lining, condensation will form. This can cause the buildup of mold and fungus inside and on the outside of the kamado or on the wooden side tables. Therefore it's important to regularly air out the cover and to check for dampness. Any leftover food in the kamado can also cause mold to

grow inside the dome and on the charcoal. The best way to get rid of these is with a high-heat burn-off.

A high-heat burn-off

It's a smart idea to burn clean the fire box once in a while at high temperature. Because no harmful organism will survive at these temperatures, a high-heat burn-off is an excellent and hygienic way of cleaning.

Place all accessories that would benefit from such a cleaning inside the kamado: the cast-iron grid, pizza stone, and/or heat shield. Over time, cast-iron grids can accumulate so much grime that ordinary brushing will have little effect. At high temperatures, all ceramics will burn white and clean.

Stoke up the kamado to 570°F (300°C). If you include accessories, a burn-off takes at least half an hour. Once it starts burning clean, close the top and bottom vents and allow the kamado and accessories to cool completely. If you wire-brush everything the next day, all the dirt will come off like dust. Afterward you will have to re-oil the cast-iron parts.

Using this method, you will keep the pizza stone, heat shield, and fire box clean and white. But through extended use, the dome will acquire a deep, dark color.

Patina

Over time, smoke and smolder will form a thin layer of carbon deposit on the inside of the dome. It's not recommended to try and burn this away, since that would require temperatures of around 930°F (500°C). At those temperatures, you risk damaging the thermometer and burning away the felt gasket. Fortunately, this patina does not have a negative effect on the working of the kamado. After a few months or a year, this carbon can start to fray and flake around the chimney. You can brush these flakes off with a wire brush to prevent pieces of carbon from falling down onto your food.

13 Cast iron maintenance

If it's possible to take out the cast-iron top vent and replace it with a ceramic lid for storage, be sure to put the vent inside the kamado. This way you don't run the risk of misplacing it. Besides, it will season as the kamado cools, which will slow down corrosion.

Usually cast-iron grids, skillets, Dutch ovens, and grill plates need to be seasoned before their first use. Some products are preseasoned (check the label); those already have a black hue. You can use them immediately, perhaps after lightly coating them with vegetable oil. We keep our grids nicely clean by brushing and oiling them continually. We prefer to use an oil with a high smoking point, like sunflower or flaxseed oil. We usually use a ball of oil-soaked paper towel to wipe off any loose grime left on the grid after brushing it. You can also brush and coat after every cooking session; this is considered good housekeeping. After a few months of use, we start over and give the grids a full high-heat burn-off (see page 54).

Cleaning the outside surface and the metal parts

Basically we never use any cleaning products on the kamado, except for on the outside. After a few smoking sessions, you will often notice brown stripes running along the dome. These are traces of liquid smoke and grease. Sauces and fats often drip along the outside of the base when you put in or take out food from the kamado. This causes stains. Once these stains burn in, they are hard to remove.

We recommend cleaning the outside of the kamado with a microfiber cloth and some general-purpose or dish soap after each use. Sometimes you will have to wait a bit until the surface has cooled off somewhat. The Grill Dome has a softer coating, which we only clean with some water, soap, and a microfiber cloth. Occasionally (once or twice a year), we spray the outside of hard-glazed ceramic kamados and metal kamados with a barbecue grill cleaner and allow the spray to absorb for five minutes. Afterward, we scrub these ceramic kamados (Big Green Egg, Primo, Kamado Joe, Monolith) with a glaze coating and a green scrubbing sponge, and metal kamados (Broil King Keg) with a microfiber cloth. Rinse off the grill cleaner with a generous amount of water.

The metal rim and hinge are made, depending on the brand, from either powder-coated or stainless steel. Both can easily be wiped with a dry cloth and some stainless-steel cleaning oil. Moving parts are best oiled with some spray lubricant like WD-40. The dome of a ceramic kamado is held in place by a tension band. It is important to check whether the band is still tight. If, through constantly heating up and cooling down, the band loosens, the dome can start to shift and even disastrously fall out. A few brands solved this by securing the band with stainless-steel clamps or by adding an extra ridge in the ceramics.

Felt replacement

Not all brands come with a special high-heat gasket, but even when they do, the material has a limited lifespan. A traditional felt gasket lasts for about a year (shorter if you make a lot of high-heat pizzas). In our catering business, a high-heat felt gasket will last about three years. Several kamado brands sell high-heat gaskets, but you can also buy Nomex "high-heat gasket" felt. Nomex is a fabric used for making fireproof clothing for race car drivers and firemen. Look for a version with an adhesive strip, because the necessary heat-resistant contact glue (3M77 Super) can be pretty expensive and is not available worldwide.

The best way to remove the old gasket is by using a paint scraper or an old hobby knife. Before you start scraping, first try to pull loose as much of the material as you can. Afterward, remove all the glue residue by first applying some acetone (it's in most nail-polish remover) and then cleaning the edge with a sponge. We prefer to see the white or yellow ceramic underneath, but as long as the edge is clean and smooth, it's fine. Let it dry for a few hours and subsequently, following the instructions on the package, install the new gasket by simply using the adhesive strip or by spraying on the special glue. Be sure not to pull the material too tightly when you apply it because when heated, Nomex will shrink. Allow the glue to dry for a day before using your kamado again.

13

CHAPTER 5
PREPARATION TECHNIQUES

Now that you understand the basic principles of lighting and regulating temperature in a kamado, it's time to apply them. In this chapter, we discuss thirteen techniques in great detail and will provide a basic recipe for each technique.

First, we will teach you all the various ways of grilling, and then we will discuss using the heat shield. As we incorporate the heat shield for recipes, we steadily increase the temperature for each dish until we're at pizza temperature. After pizza, we will discuss combination techniques and a few special techniques like "caveman style" and chicken on a vertical roaster or poultry stand.

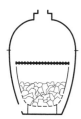

Grilling

Grilling is a technique that sparks many people's interest. Working with glowing hot coals and flames makes it appealing, and it's the most tangible way of preparing food.

At first glance, grilling is the least complicated method of preparation on a kamado. However, it actually requires the most attention, because it involves many actions in a short time span. It's easy for something to go wrong. Grilling results primarily in the Maillard reaction and caramelization (see page 37). If you're used to a different kind of grill, you'll need to unlearn a few things. As we discussed in Chapter 4, the kamado functions best with the dome closed. It's hard not to look at that great piece of grilled meat after you've just turned it over, but make sure to close the dome after every action.

Hot spots

Fill the kamado about three-quarters full with charcoal. This means up until 4 inches (10 cm) below the level of the heat shield.

The distance from the grill grid to the charcoal should be small because the glow is an important factor in browning the food, aside from the contact heat from the grid itself. If you're only grilling one or two pieces, you can make a single hot spot in the middle of the fire box. That allows you to create a specific grilling area with minimal use of charcoal. When grilling more elaborately, for more people, we like to create a triangle of heat by lighting charcoal in three places. That way you have a place on the grid outside of the triangle to gently cook the food after the initial hot contact with the grill, without any flare-ups.

Adjusting the flow

The vent positions for grilling are usually halfway open on the upper vent and three fingers wide on the bottom vent. It's best to actively regulate temperature during grilling when you notice it's going up. When the grill is in use for a long time, the temperature will increase because the dome is continuously open. In that case, restrict the airflow by further closing both vents.

We like to grill in a temperature range between 395 and 450°F (200 and 230°C) on the dome thermometer, but the dome temperature is not the only factor when grilling. To determine the correct grid temperature, we still use our hands the old-fashioned way. Hold your hand about 8 inches (20 cm) above the grid. If your hand hurts within 3 seconds, your kamado is ready to use (in that particular spot).

Optimal capacity

When you suddenly place a large amount of meat on the grill, the temperature will drop and you can allow a bit more air to come in. Make small adjustments to the top vent, leave the lower vent alone, and try not to overcompensate.

The food itself acts as a heat shield. Because the temperature decreases drastically, the food may stick to the grid. We advise you to always leave one-third of the grid empty. This aligns nicely with the use of hot spots and the triangle. A triangle of hot spots always leaves a significant part of the grid relatively cold.

Cast-iron grid techniques

When grilling, a cast-iron grid works best with a dome temperature between 390 and 460°F (200 and 240°C). In most kamados, the grid is placed about 12 inches (30 cm) above the charcoal.

The grids from the Primo and Grill Dome are placed at a greater distance from the charcoal, although these brands allow for grilling closer to the fire box with the lower grid.

Due to the radiating glow of the charcoal, the grid will be hotter than the surrounding air. Above these ideal temperatures, the grid will become too hot, and the grease that has seasoned the grid will start to smolder. You'll get black stripes on your food.

A cast-iron grid needs time to heat up. It's best to stoke up the kamado with the grid already in place. While heating it, you can brush loose the dirt and grease from the previous cooking session. A few minutes before you start grilling, you can wipe off the grid with a paper towel dipped in some vegetable oil; it should be greasy, not dripping with oil. You'll see the towel absorbs most of the dirt that you brushed loose, while simultaneously seasoning the grid, preventing the food from sticking too much.

Sizzling, sticking, and teasing

When meat or fish touches the grill grid, it should sizzle. In the places where the food makes contact with the metal, the liquid evaporates and a dark brown grill mark appears.

With a cast-iron grid, it's important not to rotate or turn over the food too fast after its first contact. Allow it to grill for at least a minute, or the food will stick to the grid and tear. The crust needs to sear, and then you can move the food more easily. But sometimes pieces stick anyway. This might happen because the grill hasn't been seasoned evenly, or the grill is too cold. Too much moisture in the food, or cooking food directly from the freezer, can also cause it to stick. The best solution is to tease the piece with tongs. Grab the meat with the tongs without actually lifting it. You can sometimes shake the piece loose by jerkily moving it sideways with your tongs. When it works, you'll notice it comes free. If it doesn't work, slide your spatula under the piece and gently lift it. Make sure to place it somewhere else, ideally on a spot where the grill is sufficiently hot.

Making grill marks

The only reason to make a grill mark is to show that the cook has given full attention to the dish. To make a nice pattern, we treat a piece of meat, poultry, or fish as follows:

- Dab the piece dry and salt it in advance.
- Place it on the grid, directly above a hot spot, listen until it sizzles, and close the lid.
- After 1 minute, rotate it 90 degrees but don't turn it over (though it's fine to peek underneath the meat).
- Wait 1 minute and turn over the meat.
- Wait 1 minute and rotate another 90 degrees.
- Wait 1 minute and take the meat off the grill.

Marking skin-on fish fillets and poultry breasts

If your fillet is lean, you can grease it lightly. Put a little oil and salt on a plate and pull the fillets through the oil. Rub off any excess oil with your hands.

First grill the flesh side to create a nice grill mark.

Ideally, use an offset or fish spatula instead of your tongs. Then place the fillet skin-side down. If the skin sticks to the grid, you can slide the fillet off its skin with your spatula once it's done. Now you still have a nice presentable side and you can pull the skin off the grid once it's baked dry. The reason to grill the flesh side of fish and poultry first is that most of its fat resides under the skin. If you grill the skin first, the risk for undesired grease smolder is greater.

Other grids besides cast iron

To achieve the same result with a standard cooking grid (stainless steel, enamel) as with cast iron, you need a higher temperature (480 to 570°F/250 to 300°C). When you use other grids, the glow and convection play the main role and the contact heat from the grid is less important. More glow, in this case, is better as it shortens the preparation time. Make sure to have a blue glowing hot spot.

With these higher temperatures, it's wise to frequently check that your food isn't burning. You should turn over the food every minute. That way you make a crust (without marks), while evenly grilling the food at the same time. If you have a lean fish, an enamel grid combined with a high temperature can be a godsend. The fish will stick less to the grid and, due to the short cooking time, it won't have a chance of drying out. With this grid, we also lightly salt and grease the fish in advance.

Grilling meat

Let's take steak as an example. The core of the meat heats up because the surrounding texture becomes hot. If there is a big difference in temperature between the outside of the meat and the core, the outside will be done sooner than the inside; there is more transition. Cell walls tear faster and moisture is drawn out and wants to evaporate.

When there is a smaller difference in temperature, the moisture will be more evenly distributed and the proteins will cook more slowly. Cell walls won't burst as fast and the result is a juicier piece of meat. In steak, the transition from brown, via gray to red or pink will be less pronounced. When the humidity under the dome is relatively high, the meat will brown more slowly. The juices in the meat won't evaporate as fast, which will yield tender meat.

We can apply this in practice by combining techniques, like grilling at hot temperatures and slow-cooking in high humidity; see page 93 for examples. With some techniques, we first heat up the outside of the steak and allow the warmth of the surface to get through to the core on the cutting board ("caveman style," see page 98). This works best with pieces that we want to serve rare.

Bones

When you have meat or fish with bones, the bone tissue plays a role in the cooking process. The way heat is transmitted by bone can be compared to ceramic in a kamado. It can take a while before bone tissue has achieved a certain temperature, but then it will transmit the heat very effectively. Because of this time delay, it is more of an issue when grilling hot and to a low temperature, like medium-rare. This is one reason why a rib steak is often more red closer to the bone.

After grilling

Depending on the thickness of the food, after you've made the grill marks, it's either ready to eat or it might need more cooking.

- **¾ to 1 inch (2 to 3 cm) thick:** Red meat will be ready to eat directly after making grill marks in the way described on page 60; measure the internal temperature or make a small cut to check that it has reached the desired temperature. Fish is almost always ready to serve immediately after grilling, but it won't hurt to check.
- **1½ to 2 inches (4 to 5 cm) thick:** When the food has reached the desired doneness, move the piece up to a spot on the grid that's less hot. If you have fish with skin, you want to place it skin-side down now; poultry should be flesh-side down after grilling. Whether you're working with a single hot spot or a triangle of hot spots, you'll need to allow space for this. Now you can continue cooking these cuts at a relatively high temperature until you are satisfied.
- **Thicker than 2 inches (5 cm):** Here we use a combination technique like a reverse sear or an initial sear (see pages 93–94).

Red meat and resting

Say you would like your steak grilled rare. If you grilled the meat on high temperature, you'll need about five minutes of resting off the heat to allow the temperature to transmit from the crust to the core of the meat. Otherwise, the meat might still be cold inside.

The advantage of allowing meat to rest after cooking is that fewer juices run from the meat when you cut it. Another function is to let the heat penetrate from the outside to the core during resting, which is called "carryover." The drawback of resting is that (and this goes for all preparations) the crust becomes softer, due to moisture exuded from the meat. This effect doubles when resting meat using foil or parchment paper—and it's a shame, as you've just put so much effort into creating a nice, tasty crust.

Allowing meat to rest is best done in a warm spot, ideally over 70°F (20°C; for example on top of your oven). Only wrap it in foil when you've really run out of options.

However, we shouldn't inflate the importance of resting meat. A number of tests have shown that meat loses between 5 and 10 percent fewer juices after resting. If, even after resting the meat for at least 10 minutes, the juices start flowing when you cut it, that is usually because the meat was frozen or refrozen.

The most important thing is not to let the juices go to waste. Collect them and make a dressing with them. Mix the meat juices with oil and spices, like a chimichurri sauce. Another way to enjoy meat juices is to serve a piece of fresh bread or a fluffy potato with your steak. You can soak up the juices and you'll get more out of your dish (many traditions have a good reason).

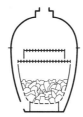

Raised grids for grilling

In most kamados the grid is placed about 12 inches (30 cm) above the charcoal, if you fill up the fire box as explained in this chapter. Occasionally, you may not want to grill fast and at high temperatures, but rather use medium heat (about 410°F/210°C) produced by glow, and most of all convection and a minimum of contact heat. This way the food will grill gradually but fast, without the crust getting burned.

This can work well for pieces that are thicker and

that we want to cook in their entirety, like meat on the bone, but also for sausages with a thin casing and bamboo skewers. It can also be great for skewers with vegetables and mushrooms, to avoid burning either the vegetables or the skewer itself.

Grilling sliced fruits and vegetables

Cutting fruits and vegetables—for example, zucchini, eggplant, pineapple, and firm tomatoes—in uniform slices will allow you to grill them in a way similar to fish or steak. You can even do it simultaneously with meat on the grill.

Lightly grease vegetables with oil and season them with salt; we often sprinkle sugar on fruits instead, as this dehydrates the surface, just like salt does for other foods. Make a crosshatch grill pattern, ideally on a clean cast-iron grid, and cook until the food is as tender as you'd like.

We add dressing and marinades on the plates after removing vegetables and fruit from the grill. This prevents flare-ups and ensures a nice caramelized crust. Once they're on a plate, the warm produce will nicely absorb the taste of the dressing.

Grilling shellfish and crustaceans

For grilling shellfish and crustaceans, we like to use a flat grill wok or grill basket on top of the standard grid for smaller seafood. This is a perforated, enameled grid with holes that prevent the shells and shrimp from falling through the cracks. If you don't have a grill wok, you can achieve the same effect by crossing two grids.

Smaller shellfish

Over the years, we've tried grilling all sorts of shellfish. You can prepare smaller shells like mussels, cockles, venus clams, and razor clams by the pound using a grill basket. The preparation carries a small risk, as a good amount of steam can escape when you open the kamado. The first shells open due to the dry heat, the juice drips on top of the charcoal, and the rest of the shells steam open as a domino effect. Wear gloves and cover your forearms completely. You can use a towel to carefully open the lid. The large amount of moisture and salt in this technique would make a cast-iron grid corrode very soon; it's best to use an enamel grid.

- Rinse out the shells for about 10 minutes in slowly running water to remove all sand.
- Throw out open or broken shells.
- Fire up the kamado to 425°F (220°C) with a standard grid and grill wok or basket.
- Create a large hot spot or triangle directly under the grill wok.
- Spread the shells out over the wok and close the kamado.
- Wait 3 to 4 minutes before opening the kamado. It can now steam heavily.
- Carefully open the kamado with a dishcloth and check if all the shells have opened. Take tongs or a long spoon and stir the shells, as sometimes they'll open that way.
- If not all the shells are open, close the kamado and wait at least another minute.
- Repeat, if necessary.
- Some shells don't want to open at all; you should throw those out.
- If all the shells have opened, take the entire grill wok out of the kamado.
- Remove the shellfish to a bowl and serve.

We like to serve these when they've just opened, but for others this may be too raw. You can choose to cook them for another minute after all the shells have opened.

Larger shellfish

The preparation of oysters, clams, pullet carpet shells, and large razor clams is about the same as for small shellfish. However, if we wait until the shells open completely by themselves, the meat will be overdone and chewy. Instead, remove the grill wok from the kamado once they're warm and use an oyster knife to pry them open. A clam opens just a bit, after which we cut it in half with a chef's knife. You don't really need a grill wok to grill large shellfish, but it's just easier to help lift the shells out of the kamado in one swift movement.

- Fire up the kamado to 425°F (220°C) with one large hot spot.
- To test, place a single shell bottom-side down (if you can determine which side that is) on the grid.
- Wait, with the dome closed, for about 3 minutes.

- Every shell requires its own specific preparation. Open the kamado:
  - Feel the top of an oyster. If it's ready, it will feel warm and you can pry it open with an oyster knife.
  - You can open up clams and pullet carpet shells once they've just cracked open. The meat may still be tender.
  - With large razor clams, the two halves will fall apart and the tube of meat will fall out. Cut the meat loose where it's fastened to the shell. You can now continue cooking the razor clams on the grill or in a skillet.
- After the first shell, you know the preparation time and you can grill several at once. Throw out any shells that do not open.
- Remove the shellfish to a bowl and serve.

Shrimp

Prepare shrimp at a temperature of 425°F (220°C) with a triangle of hot spots. For smaller shrimp, a grill wok is ideal. You can mix shrimp with vegetables, spices, and garlic for a complete meal.

Remove the digestive tract if this hasn't been done already. Ideally use shrimp in the shell as they'll be juicier. It doesn't matter much for the taste if the shell becomes quite dark from sugars in a marinade. Once the shrimp is pink-orange all around, it should be ready. If you wish, you can slice one open to check. Remove the shrimp to a platter and serve.

Large crustaceans: lobsters, spiny lobsters, and king crabs

Halve live or raw crustaceans lengthwise with a knife (you can also ask your fishmonger to do this).

- Rinse the lobster or spiny lobster thoroughly to remove the digestive tract and the intestines. We do this because they would fall out of the shell or stick to the grid otherwise.
- Fire up the kamado to 425°F (220°C) with one large hot spot.
- Dab the meat side dry and place a halved, cleaned lobstertail, meat-side down, on the grid. Create a grill mark.
- Turn the half over and cook it shell-side down. Press the meat to determine how done it is; once the meat is firm and doesn't give, it's ready. The shell's color should be deep red. Another sign that the lobster is ready: when steam escapes from the elbows of its claws and joints.

Grill the claws of a lobster separately (the langoustine doesn't have them). They need to cook as long, or even a little longer than the lobster half. Prepare king crab claws in the same way as lobster claws. The difference is their size, and the color is not as important. An entire claw will only fit on the largest grills, so you'll usually work in batches.

Always cut the king crab claws open to check if they've cooked nicely. Experience or guidance is important, but the meat should be firm like a well-done steak. Our experience is that the parts of the claws that were connected to the body usually need more time than the outer claws.

Grilled Entrecôte or Strip Steak

The quality of the beef is very important for this simple preparation. We like to use aged and marbled beef such as Choice or Prime. The thickness of the meat matters when grilling; this particular recipe will give you a medium-rare steak.

· Fire up the kamado with the cast-iron grid to 395°F (200°C) and create four hot spots.
· Sprinkle the beef with a generous amount of salt and pepper and rub it into the meat.
· While cooking, close the lid after each action. Place each piece of beef on a hot spot on the grid for 90 seconds, then rotate it 90 degrees. Grill for another 90 seconds. Turn over the meat, grill for another 90 seconds, and rotate the meat again 90 degrees. Grill for another 90 seconds. Both sides should now have perfect grill marks.

· Continue to cook until the steaks reach the desired degree of doneness. Most steaks will cook to an internal temperature of 125°F (50 to 52°C) for rare if you follow this recipe, taking the steak directly out of the fridge before grilling, or 130°F (55°C) for medium if you take it out at least half an hour before grilling.
· Let the meat rest off the grill for a few minutes in a warm area before you cut it.

TIP *Grilled shallots are delicious with grilled beef. Halve 4 shallots (with skin) and grill them alongside the meat. Place them cut-side down on top of the beef for the last 4 minutes of grilling. When the shallots are tender, remove the skin and serve them with the beef.*

SERVES 4

· 4 (8-ounce/225-g) entrecôtes/ strip steaks, 1 1/4 inches (3 cm) thick
· Coarse sea salt
· Freshly ground black pepper

WHAT YOU NEED
· Cast-iron grid
· Food thermometer

TEMPERATURE
· 395°F (200°C)

Grilled Entrecôte or Strip Steak

Grilled Clams and Cockles

You can get both kinds of shellfish throughout most of the year, but they are best from late fall until early summer. Cockles are sweeter than clams and have more meat; clams have a more pronounced taste. The shells should smell of fresh seawater when you buy them. If they have an unpleasant smell and the bag is slimy when you grab it, don't buy them.

Rinsing the sand from between the shells is very important. You can do this by soaking them in clean, salted water before cooking. The shells will open up and spit out the sand. This recipe can easily be ruined by getting sand between your teeth when you eat the shellfish. We sometimes ask our fishmonger to place a net of shellfish in the lobster basin overnight. That way you get them superclean.

· Dissolve the salt in 2 quarts (2 L) of clean water and divide it between two containers.
· Place each kind of shellfish in a container with the salted water. Let them rest for at least 15 minutes, then rinse them twice under running water.

· Fire up the kamado with the grid to 425°F (220°C) and create three hot spots. Place the grill wok on the grid and wait until it is hot.
· Place the clams in the wok first as they usually need a little longer to open up than the cockles. Place the cockles in the wok about half a minute later and close the lid.
· Check after about 2 minutes whether all the shells are open by stirring them with a slotted spoon or tongs. If you like your shellfish nearly raw, take the wok out of the kamado once they've just opened up. If you want them cooked thoroughly, grill them for another 1 to 2 minutes. When you grill them for too long, you risk the meat becoming tough.
· Scoop the shellfish into a deep bowl. Season them with a grind of pepper and sprinkle them with the parsley. The shellfish remain quite salty during cooking, so there's no need to add salt.

TIP *This is a basic recipe that can, of course, be varied endlessly with garlic oil, dressings, and mayonnaises.*

SERVES 4 AS A STARTER

- 3 tablespoons table salt
- 2 pounds (1 kg) venus clams
- 2 pounds (1 kg) cockles
- Freshly ground black pepper
- A few tablespoons julienned fresh flat-leaf parsley

WHAT YOU NEED

- Standard grid
- Grill wok with holes

TEMPERATURE

- 425°F (220°C)

Grilled Clams and Cockles

Grilled Lobster with Lime Mayonnaise

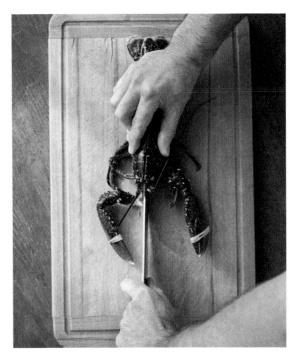

Grilled Lobster with Lime Mayonnaise

While boiling or steaming may be the more common ways to prepare lobster, we prefer to grill them. We find that grilling makes lobsters take on an intense, smoky flavor you wouldn't get from boiling them. Served with lime mayonnaise, this dish is perfect for a summer cookout.

· Fire up the kamado with the cast-iron grid to 425°F (220°C) and create three hot spots.

· Prepare the mayonnaise: You can prepare the mayonnaise a few hours in advance. In a stand mixer fitted with the whisk attachment, combine the egg yolks, lime zest and juice, mustard, Worcestershire, and confectioners' sugar. Turn on the machine and slowly pour in the oil until you achieve the right texture. Add the salt and pepper to taste. Pour the sauce into a clean jar, screw the lid on, and refrigerate it. The mayonnaise will keep in the refrigerator for 3 to 5 days.

· Meanwhile, halve the lobsters. When working with live lobsters, it's important to kill them as humanely as possible. Place the tip of a large cooking knife just behind the head of the lobster and cleave its head lengthwise in one fast movement. Continue by cutting the entire lobster in half. Remove the intestines by rinsing the lobster.

· Dab the meat dry and grease it lightly with oil. Sprinkle with salt. Don't forget to remove the rubber bands from the claws.

· Place the lobster halves meat-side down on the grid and grill them for about 4 minutes. Turn the lobsters over and grill them on their shell sides for another 5 minutes. Close the lid after each action. The meat in the tail may remain a little glassy. Press the meat to determine how done it is; once the meat is firm and doesn't give, it's ready. The shell's color should be deep red. You can also tell that the lobster is ready when steam escapes from the elbows of its claws and joints.

· Take the lobsters off the grid and gently break open the claws with a meat hammer or a firm cooking knife. Season them with salt and pepper and serve them with the mayonnaise.

TIP *You can prepare the claws of a North Sea crab in the same way. The total cooking time will be about 12 minutes. You can vary the mayonnaise by seasoning it with lemon zest and juice instead of lime.*

SERVES 4

FOR THE MAYONNAISE
· 2 egg yolks
· Finely grated zest and juice of 1 lime
· 1 teaspoon Dijon mustard
· 1 teaspoon Worcestershire sauce
· 1 teaspoon confectioners' sugar
· About 7 ounces (200 ml) sunflower oil
· 3/4 teaspoon sea salt
· Freshly ground black pepper

FOR THE LOBSTER
· 2 (14-ounce to 1 1/4-pound/ 400- to 600-g) lobsters, preferably live
· Sunflower oil, for greasing
· Sea salt
· Freshly ground black pepper

WHAT YOU NEED
· Cast-iron grid

TEMPERATURE
· 425°F (220°C)

Indirect cooking

Using the heat shield at low and high temperatures

The kamado can be used as an oven and smoker with indirect cooking methods. Without the heat shield, the kamado is no more than a very good, expensive grill. The heat shield creates a space in the kamado in which one can control a constant temperature. This can be as low as 120°F (50°C) and as high as 660°F (350°C), depending on the technique. (If you have a Primo Oval, the heat shield consists of both of the D-shields.)

Within this chapter, we will slowly increase the grill temperature with each technique. We first tackle smoking fish and slow-cooking. Then we talk about breads and desserts, and finally master baking a pizza. After learning these four techniques, you will be able to apply this knowledge to all kinds of indirect cooking techniques with varying temperatures.

Placing the heat shield

In the illustration, you'll see the standard position for indirect cooking. The charcoal fills the fire box up until about 6 inches (15 cm) below the heat shield. That space is needed to allow airflow over the charcoal. If your box is too full and the charcoal touches the heat shield, you'll get smoke. The heat shield is most effective at the lowest position, because that allows the most workspace beneath the dome.

A metal drip pan is never a bad idea. It collects grease and meat juices, allowing your heat shield to remain clean. If, after a low temperature exercise you want to really fire up the kamado, a dirty heat shield can have some rather unpleasant fumes. In most cases, a heat shield lowers the dome temperature by about 90°F (50°C). The heat shield reduces most of the glow and part of the convection.

Slow-cooking meat and fish

When you're using a low temperature in the kamado, the proteins in the meat and fish will coagulate more evenly. We're talking about a dome temperature between 160 and 250°F (70 and 120°C). The fat content in the main ingredient is vital in this case, to keep the food moist as it cooks. The rule of thumb is: The higher the fat content, the longer you can cook it. This is crucial in cheaper cuts of meat, because they contain tougher fibers that need to break down in order to make them palatable. By slow-cooking, we alter the connective tissue into easily digestible and succulent gelatin. For fish, we use a relatively short cooking time, because it contains less tough tissue. If you cook fish too fast and at too high a temperature, you'll easily overcook it and it will taste dry.

Hot smoking

Hot smoking means slowly or gently cooking with wood smoke below 212°F (100°C) but above 100°F (40°C). Smoking at temperatures under 100°F (40°C) is called cold smoking. As a technique, hot smoking lends itself well to fish fillets or whole fish—but also to poultry fillets and pieces of game and lamb. These are delicate pieces with a refined taste. The cooking time is between 10 and 45 minutes. For this technique, you should only place the heat shield after you've placed the smoking wood in the kamado. It is impractical to constantly lift the heat shield from the kamado to add smoking wood. (Monolith has found a solution for this by making an opening in the exterior of the kamado and a slit to drop in wood chips on top of the charcoal.)

Amount of smoking wood

Because we often hot smoke delicate pieces of meat and fish, it's important to take it a little easy with the quantity of smoking wood. Less is more, in this case.

The amount of smoking wood depends more on the time you need to prepare the food than the number of ingredients you have under the dome. Chunks will give a constant, longer smoking time. For most fish fillets, a single chunk of 4 inches (10 cm) should be enough. For a longer session, for a pork neck or a boston butt, we use several chunks that we place in the vicinity of the hot spot. This also works with wood chips. Chips will immediately give off a good puff of smoke. For a few fish fillets, a small handful is more than enough. If you scatter the wood chips, you can smoke repeatedly during long sessions. The burning charcoal will regularly "find" new pieces of smoking wood.

Adjusting the temperature for hot smoking

For hot smoking at 175°F (80°C), you need to light the kamado with a single hot spot. Allow the temperature to increase over about 10 minutes to 250°F (120°C) with a half-open top and two fingers wide bottom vent. Throw the smoking wood on the hot spot and put the heat shield and the drip pan in place. Now swiftly place an ingredient on any grid you wish. Wait before closing the dome until you have seen the first smoke curl around the heat shield. The cold ingredient forms an obstruction and will lower the dome temperature. The temperature will first end up between 120 and 160°F (50 and 70°C). The low temperature is a bonus, as smoke flavors are more easily absorbed into the fish or meat. Immedi-

ately start tempering the airflow by reducing the openings to just a crack in the top and bottom vents. After about 5 minutes, the temperature will find a balance. Now you can decide whether or not to allow in more air. A good rule of thumb for hot smoking is: The lower the dome temperature, and therefore the longer the cooking time, the better your result.

If, in the first 10 minutes, the dome temperature doesn't exceed 120°F (50°C), you may want to test whether warm air escapes from the top vent (you'll see it if smoke keeps leaking out). A thin blue sliver of smoke is ideal. If your time is limited and you want to cook faster, allow more air in until the temperature stabilizes around 175 to 200°F (80 to 90°C). Just make sure the dome temperature doesn't exceed 212°F (100°C). It won't affect the texture and taste so much, but the fish won't look as pretty. Use a probe thermometer to determine the right temperature. If you're preparing fillets, your fish begins to cook when clear liquid pours out where you poked the thermometer. Once this liquid is white and solidified, the fish is usually ready, depending on its thickness.

Slow-cooking

This technique is used for larger pieces of meat that require a longer cooking time, and for combination techniques like initial sear and end sear (see pages 93–94).

The differences between hot smoking and slow-cooking meat are that the temperature for slow-cooking is higher between 225 and 280°F (110 and 140°C), and that we usually fill the drip pan with water. The positioning and method are otherwise the same. Cooking times can vary between 30 minutes and 12 hours. If you add wood smoke during slow-cooking, you've wandered into the territory of American barbecue.

American barbecue is the tradition of slowly cooking large cuts of meat with smoke. This is generally done at about 225°F (110°C). While we enjoy making American barbeque and love eating it, you won't see any recipes in this book. We leave the description of different techniques, marinades, and sauces to our American colleagues. We really liked *Big Bob Gibson's BBQ Book* by Chris Lilly.

However, the techniques described here can very well be applied to American barbecue. The kamado is perfectly suited for these methods, and you'll often see kamados at barbecue competitions in America and in Europe.

Humidity

For slow-cooking meat, we often use a drip pan filled with water because usually more grease and juices drip down with the sugars of a rub or marinade, but that is not the only reason. When you're slow-cooking meat, controlling the humidity within the dome is quite important. It's easy to reach an ideal humidity of more than 10 percent. Ingredients will cook faster and more evenly and won't dehydrate as much. The meat juices won't evaporate as fast in a humid environment. Depending on the recipe, you can use the following techniques:

- **A water pan:** This is the most simple and effective way to control the humidity. When you're done cooking, you can let the pan cook dry to encourage more of a Maillard reaction (see page 38).
- **Spray:** You can spray the meat occasionally with apple juice, beer, water, or a little whiskey. We use a plastic spray bottle. We use this technique a lot when preparing spare ribs; we spray them for the last 30 minutes of a 5-hour cooking time.

- **Glazing:** You can brush with a sauce right before serving. It can freshen up a dry crust and make it less tough.
- **Wrapping in aluminum foil:** This technique is used a lot during grilling contests. In our experience, this is usually not necessary in a kamado as it's a humidity-controlled environment.

Adjusting the temperature for slow-cooking

For slow-cooking, the dome temperature can be above 212°F (100°C). The upper limit is about 285°F (140°C); any higher and it becomes more like an oven. It's important to adjust in small increments. It's fine to start at a lower temperature than indicated, and if you're adding smoke, it's actually beneficial to start low because that aids with smoke penetration. It requires some patience to control the temperature over the course of several hours of cooking. Only after 5 to 10 minutes will you see the effects of small tweaks in the airflow on the temperature.

If you're more experienced, there's no need to constantly stay with the kamado. Don't go shopping for an hour the first time, but take a peek every 15 minutes. If necessary, make a small adjustment and go do something else.

In this case, a probe thermometer with a wire and alarm comes in handy. This way, you can monitor the cooking process. There are also devices that monitor the temperature via a dome thermometer and a probe thermometer, and they operate via radio, Wi-Fi, or Bluetooth. The ultimate device is a PID controller that not only registers temperatures but also intervenes when the temperature drops. A fan mounted on the lower vent then blows in air to increase the temperature. These are pricey solutions, but very useful when you're cooking for up to 12 hours.

Raised grids

The advantage of using a raised grid for low-temperature techniques is that hot air and smoke can be evenly distributed around the ingredient. The ingredient is positioned close to the dome thermometer, so the

measurement is more precise. Just make sure the dome thermometer doesn't poke into your meat or fish, as it will show a lower temperature.

Baking bread, desserts, and pizza

We've long been convinced that bread and pizza can be baked in the same setup within the kamado, but it was when we were developing this book that we changed our minds. (We'll explain when we get to actually baking the pizza.) Let's talk about the dough first.

Everything you learn to do by hand only goes easier with a machine. This is especially the case with bread and pizza dough. In our recipes, we assume that you have a stand mixer with a dough hook.

For your first attempts to bake bread or pizza dough, you can use a bread machine and store-bought bread mix or pizza mix. Many machines have a setting for kneading the dough for about 90 minutes. This means you have your hands free to practice with the kamado.

Setup for bread and desserts

For most of the recipes in this chapter, a greasy, smoky, or grill flavor isn't desirable. The light aroma of a wood stove is fine, but we want the kamado to burn as cleanly as possible. This means that the heat shield and the pizza stone need to be clean.

Pay extra attention to the quality of your charcoal, and make sure to work with nice large lumps. If there's a lot of ash and small pieces in the fire box, scoop it out (before lighting) and select the charcoal by hand. The setup is the same as for slow-cooking, with the addition of a pizza stone: the heat shield is in the low position, with the grid above it with some space in between. In some cases, a drip pan also comes in handy (for steaming during the final oven spring).

Firing up and controlling oven temperature for baking

After filling the fire box, light up three fire starters in the middle of the charcoal. This way, you'll get an intense hot spot that is shielded by the heat shield. As soon as the fire starters are completely burned (in this case, very important), you can place the heat shield directly over the glow. If you're planning on baking bread, a small drip pan may come in handy. Place the standard grid and keep the pizza stone aside for a while.

Depending on the recipe, stoke up the kamado for about 20 minutes to 355 to 450°F (180 to 230°C). Once you've reached the desired dome temperature, this doesn't necessarily mean there is enough heat within the ceramic. Take your time and let the ceramic heat up. The more reflection from the dome, the better your crust will be. Place the pizza stone on the grid and allow another 15 minutes for everything to get back to the desired temperature.

Baking artisanal bread

Once the dough has completely risen and is in the right shape, you can bake it. Small rolls are easier than large 1-pound (500-g) loaves, but baking your first large loaf on a kamado is very satisfying.

- Gently lift the pizza stone and pour half a glass of water in the drip pan. This will evaporate and will help the oven spring during the first 10 minutes, without the crust immediately tearing apart.
- Dust the stone lightly with flour or use parchment paper to prevent the bread from sticking.
- Position the dough in the middle of the pizza stone.
- If the temperature suddenly drops because you just put cold dough in the kamado, raise the temperature by allowing more air in during the first 10 minutes.
- Leave the bread alone for at least 10 minutes.
- You may peek through the chimney, but keep the lid closed.
- Open the dome after 10 minutes and rotate the bread 90 degrees. This way, you can also check that the bread doesn't stick and that the bottom isn't burning.
- Make sure the temperature in the kamado isn't higher than you want; it may even stay a bit below. This is to guarantee that the bread can bake evenly.
- If the bottom of the bread becomes too dark because the stone is too hot, turn the bread over, or use a raised grid to allow the bread to finish without burning it.
- When there's a crust on the bottom and the bread feels hollow when you knock on it, these are signs the bread is done. Stick to the baking time as indicated in the recipe.
- Now the hardest part: Let the bread cool off and release a little steam on a wire rack for at least half an hour (ideally an hour) before you cut it.

Baking desserts

We usually make desserts in the kamado in a cake tin or springform pan. Silicone baking sheets also work perfectly in a kamado. You would think that the pizza stone has no function in this case, but it helps to control temperature. It prevents the bottom of your tart or cake from burning. This is why we use the same setup as for bread. An exception for this is dishes such as crème brûlée (and pâté); for those, we place a water pan on top of the standard grid and we stoke the heat in the same way as when slow-cooking.

Baking pizza

This technique is suitable for all flat breads: pizza, naan, *pide*, and *flammkuchen*. The set-up of the grids, heat shields, and pizza stones varies per brand of kamado, but the principle is the same. Always work with a heat shield and a pizza stone. Ideally don't place the two stones on top of each other, as there's the chance that the bottom of your pizza will burn. There should be as much space between the edge of the fire box and the heat shield as possible. We like to place the pizza stone as high up in the dome and far away from the charcoal as possible, without limiting the convection. This is to create maximum convection in the dome, without the glow making the bottom of the pizza stone too hot.

In the photo opposite, you can see examples of a few brands. For Monolith, Kamado Joe (models before 2014), and most Chinese manufacturers, turn the grid upside down and slide the heat shield on the metal triangle. Place the pizza stone on the three legs in which you normally place the heat shield. With the Grill Dome, we place a stone as the heat shield on the grid and flip the indirect grid upside down, on top of which we place a second pizza stone to bake on. With the Primo, you can do more or less the same by placing the D-Plates on the standard grid and the pizza stone on the raised grid. With the Big Green Egg, we flip the convEGGtor upside down and use something to create a small space in between the two stones. In the photo, we've used a grid from a different, smaller model to create more space.

Charcoal selection and firing up high

To reach the temperature needed for baking pizza, you need a good selection of charcoal. You need to get to a temperature of more than 570°F (300°C). At this temperature and higher, the dough rises very quickly, makes big air bubbles, and quickly becomes crispy. Between 610 and 680°F (320 and 360°C) is ideal for Italian pizza, but some pizza purists will try as high as 700°F (370°C). The kamado does get very hot; be careful if there are children running around. Make sure to check your warranty, too, as some gaskets don't last long if you heat to these temperatures frequently. To prepare the kamado:

- Clean the fire box and make sure the air holes are open.
- Fill the fire box with the nicest, largest lumps of charcoal from the bag. That way there will be maximum airflow between the lumps.
- Light four fire starters, scattered over the charcoal.
- Heat the kamado up to 300°F (150°C), and once the charcoal glows, open all the vents completely.
- Place the heat shield.
- Heat the kamado up to 480°F (250°C) with the heat shield. This can take about half an hour.
- Place the pizza stone and heat it up to at least 610°F (320°C). All charcoal should be glowing red at this point.

Now the kamado is ready for the pizza. The time between lighting and heating up may be 45 minutes to an hour. The charcoal burns very quickly now, so there is usually only about 45 minutes to an hour to bake. The temperature will then drop to 480 to 525°F (250 to 275°C). This is still hot enough to bake pizza (like the recipe we give on page 138), but the crust will get a softer, more of a risen dough structure, with smaller air bubbles like in bread. We prefer thin crust, so we try to bake at a higher temperature.

Important tips

When you're first making pizza in a kamado, it's best to use as few toppings as possible. The first pizza sometimes doesn't work because the temperature is too cold or too hot. Sprinkling coarse cornmeal (polenta) on the pizza stone prevents the crust from burning and allows it to come off more easily. If the cornmeal burns immediately, you'll know that the stone is too hot. In that case, you can take it out of the kamado with a glove and double-folded dishcloth. Another trick is to wipe off the stone with a thick wet cloth. When you're done baking pizza, leave all accessories in the kamado. They are often too hot to handle, so it's best to let them cool off in the kamado.

PIZZA SETUPS FROM TOP TO BOTTOM: **KAMADO JOE (MODELS BEFORE 2014, ALSO APPLIES TO MONOLITH), BIG GREEN EGG, GRILL DOME.**

Wood-Smoked Haddock

Haddock can easily be hot smoked just like salmon, trout, and sturgeon (to name a few of our favorites.) Like its relative the cod, haddock is a fragile fish, especially the larger fillets that have a looser texture. Therefore, we prefer to work with small fillets with the skin on. You can substitute cod, trout, or other white-fish fillets, if you'd like.

· Dab the fillets dry with paper towels. Sprinkle them with salt and pepper.
· Fire up the kamado to 250 to 265°F (120 to 130°C) and create a single hot spot.
· Drop a handful of wood chips, or place a single chunk, directly on top of the hot spot. Place the heat shield, the empty drip pan, and the grid in place.
· Place the fillets, skin-side down, on the grid. Once you see smoke spiraling up around the edge of the heat shield, close the lid.

· Now the temperature inside the kamado will decrease to about 175°F (80°C). Try to stabilize this temperature. You'll achieve the best result by making sure the temperature stays below 212°F (100°C), otherwise the fish may start sweating, which will cover it in a white film.
· Smoke the fillets for approximately 25 minutes, or until they reach an internal temperature of 120°F (48°C).

TIP *Serve this smoked haddock fillet with a delicious tarragon cream. Simply stir 1 tablespoon minced fresh tarragon into 7 ounces (200 g) sour cream and then season it with a pinch each of salt and pepper.*

SERVES 4

· 4 (4 1/4-to-5 1/4-ounce/ 120-to-150-g) haddock fillets, preferably skin-on
· Coarse sea salt
· Freshly ground black pepper

WHAT YOU NEED

· Whiskey barrel smoking wood (chips or chunks)
· Heat shield
· Drip pan
· Standard grid
· Food thermometer

TEMPERATURE

· 175°F (80°C)

Wood-Smoked Haddock

Slow-Cooked Pork Neck

Slow-Cooked Pork Neck

Boneless pork neck was originally the least expensive part of the pig. This was because of its high fat content and many membranes—but those are what make it perfectly suited for slow-cooking. In recent years, pork neck has been made so popular by grillers that you pay almost as much for it now as for the fillet. This is mostly the case with free-range pigs like the Mangalitsa, Ibérico, and Duke of Berkshire. Just as with beef, the breeds of pig available keep expanding, though good pork is usually best bought locally.

With this technique, you will achieve a deliciously juicy and tender result. This is a roast that is excellent for a large group—for a Sunday cookout, for example. Serve it with bread or roasted potatoes, crème fraîche, and mustard.

· Fire up the kamado with the heat shield, the drip pan filled with water, and the standard grid in place to 225°F (110°C) and create a single hot spot.
· In a small bowl, mix the garlic, rosemary, both mustards, and the honey. Add the salt and pepper to taste.
· With a sharp knife, slice a pocket into the meat lengthwise, no more than three-quarters deep. Leave the ends intact. Pull the meat open and make another, angled cut halfway into this pocket (see first photo on page 85) to allow the flavor of the filling to be absorbed everywhere.
· Stuff the meat with the mustard and herb mix.
· Bind the neck back together with butcher's twine. A butcher's knot looks good, but three strings with a bow work just as well. Place the bay leaves on top of the pork neck or stick them under the twine.
· Sprinkle the exterior of the pork neck with salt and pepper. If there's filling leftover, you can rub the meat with it.
· Place the meat on the grid, close the lid, and cook for about 3 hours, until the meat has reached an internal temperature of 145 to 153°F (63 to 67°C).
· In the last 20 to 30 minutes, you can stoke up the temperature to 300°F (150°C) so the crust can obtain more color and flavor.
· Remove the roast and cut it into thick slices.

TIP *When you start cooking, place a chunk of apple wood on the charcoal for a deeper color and a light smoky taste.*

SERVES 10

· 4 cloves garlic, minced
· 1 sprig fresh rosemary, leaves minced
· 2 tablespoons coarse mustard
· 1 tablespoon Dijon mustard
· 2 tablespoons acacia or flower honey
· 1 teaspoon coarse sea salt
· Freshly ground black pepper
· 4 1/2 pounds (2 kg) boneless pork neck
· 6 fresh bay leaves

WHAT YOU NEED

· Heat shield
· Drip pan
· Standard grid
· Butcher's twine
· Food thermometer

TEMPERATURE

· 225 to 300°F (110 to 150°C)

Pizza Margherita

This is the best example of the original, thin-crust pizza from Naples. Our finest hour was working with a real *pizzaiolo* to test if Jeroen's original Big Green Egg could produce a good pizza with their ingredients. It did.

· Make the dough: Pour the water in the bowl of a stand mixer fitted with a dough hook. Add 3 heaping tablespoons of the flour and the yeast. Stir and let them stand for a few minutes to activate the yeast.

· Turn the machine on to medium speed and add, spoon by spoon, the rest of the flour. Let it mix for 10 to 15 minutes, until the dough is firm and elastic but still a bit sticky.

· Add the salt and mix for another 2 minutes. Cover the bowl with a moist towel and let the dough rise for 2 hours at room temperature, until it has doubled in size.

· On a lightly floured work surface, flatten the dough into its original size. Divide the dough into four equal portions, shape into balls, and place them on parchment paper. Let the balls rise, covered with a moist towel, for 4 hours at room temperature.

· Prepare the toppings: In a medium pan, sauté the garlic in the oil over medium heat. Add the tomatoes and oregano. Simmer for 25 minutes, until the tomatoes fall apart. Press the sauce through a fine-mesh sieve, pour the solids back into the pan, and season with salt and pepper. Set aside to cool.

· Make the pizza: Fire up the kamado with the heat shield and raised grid to at least 610°F (320°C).

· Place the pizza stone on the grid or rack of the heat shield about 15 minutes before baking.

· Remove one of the dough balls from under the towel. It requires some practice to shape the dough by hand—as an alternative, use a rolling pin on a flour-dusted counter. Use your thumbs to push the dough slightly upward at the edges. Make sure that the diameter of the dough fits the pizza stone.

· Sprinkle the pizza peel with flour and arrange the dough on it.

· Scoop a spoonful of sauce onto the dough. Spread with the back of the spoon, circling from inside outward, without touching the edge of the crust. Brush oil around the edge and arrange one-quarter of the cheese over the sauce.

· Sprinkle the pizza stone with the cornmeal. Slide the pizza gently onto the pizza stone. Close the lid and bake it for 3 minutes.

· Carefully open the kamado and peek under the dough to see if the crust is dark in spots; the pizza may be done already. If not, close the lid and check after 2 minutes. If not, continue baking and check every minute. Take the pizza off the stone when the bottom is brown, the crust is risen, and the mozzarella is bubbly. Sprinkle with a handful of torn basil and serve.

· Repeat with the remaining dough and toppings.

MAKES 4 PIZZAS

FOR THE DOUGH
- 9 ounces (275 ml) cold water
- 3 3/4 cups (500 g) all-purpose flour, plus more for dusting
- 1 teaspoon dry yeast
- 1 tablespoon coarse sea salt

FOR THE TOPPINGS
- 2 cloves garlic, sliced
- 1 tablespoon olive oil, plus more for brushing
- 2 (14-ounce/400-g) cans peeled tomatoes, drained
- 1 tablespoon chopped fresh oregano
- Sea salt
- Freshly ground black pepper
- 2 (8 3/4-ounce/250-g) balls buffalo mozzarella, drained and torn into 1-inch (2.5-cm) pieces
- 1/2 cup (70 g) coarse cornmeal
- 1 bunch fresh basil, torn

WHAT YOU NEED
- Heat shield
- Raised grid
- Pizza stone
- Pizza peel

TEMPERATURE
- 610 to 680°F (320 to 360°C)

TIP *You can vary the ingredients for toppings endlessly.*

Pizza Margherita

White Bread Rolls

White Bread Rolls

There is nothing more satisfying than making your own bread. This most simple of bread recipes can deliver a very satisfying result: a crusty and fluffy bread roll. The kamado provides the crust; the repeated leavening cycles produce the air inside the dough and the sweet flavor. We start you off with rolls, because they are a little easier than a large bread loaf, but you can use these same ingredients and work them into a large loaf as described on page 132.

· Mix the flour, yeast, salt, and water in a stand mixer fitted with a dough hook until they form a smooth, cohesive dough. Add the oil at the last moment. Check with a food thermometer that the dough has a temperature of 80°F (25°C) so that it will rise well. If the temperature is lower, knead some more.

· Place the dough on the counter on top of a clean, flour-dusted dishcloth. Lay another clean, flour-dusted dishcloth over the dough (flour-side down) and cover it all with plastic wrap. Allow to rise for 1 to 2 hours.

· Divide the dough into four equal balls about 3½ ounces (100 g) each.

Position the balls on top of and under the dishcloths, cover with plastic wrap, and let rise for another 30 minutes.

· Press the air from the dough balls, shape into the desired form, and place them between the dishcloths again. Cover with the plastic wrap and let rise for 2 more hours.

· Fire up the kamado with the heat shield and standard grid to 425°F (220°C). Place the pizza stone on the grid or on the rack of the heat shield about 15 minutes before you start baking. Close the dome and let it get back to 425°F (220°C).

· With a sharp knife, carve shallow crosses in the tops of the buns. This will give the bread some space to expand while it's baking.

· Dust the pizza stone with flour. Put the buns on the stone and bake for about 25 minutes, or until golden brown with a crispy crust.

MAKES 4 ROLLS

- 3 cups (420 g) bread flour, plus more for dusting
- 1 teaspoon dry yeast
- 1½ teaspoons fine sea salt
- 1 cup (240 ml) warm water (at 110 to 115°F/43 to 46°C)
- ½ teaspoon olive oil

WHAT YOU NEED

- Food thermometer
- Heat shield
- Standard grid
- Pizza stone

TEMPERATURE

- 425°F (220°C)

TIP *You can use this recipe to make delicious bread with grains and seeds or with nuts. Add, after you've mixed in the olive oil, ¼ cup (30 g) sunflower seeds, ¼ cup (30 g) pumpkin seeds, and 3 tablespoons flax seeds to the dough. For nuts, add, after mixing in the olive oil, ⅓ cup (40 g) each coarsely chopped toasted hazelnuts and walnuts to the dough. Knead the dough just until they are incorporated and continue as described above.*

Combination techniques

After learning these techniques, you can apply your knowledge to all indirect preparations with differing temperatures. Say you'd like to cook a nice, thick piece of meat or an entire fish. With just grilling, it's hard to get the desired result. With slow-cooking you will get a nice internal texture, but it lacks the Maillard reaction and therefore flavor. And of course it's absolutely fine to use an oven preparation of between 300 and 360°F (150 and 180°C), which is what we often do for whole birds like chickens and turkeys. The hot air does most of the work. There is still a chance, though, that it will cook too quickly and the interior meat will turn dry, or the meat will cook nicely but lack a good crust. Instead, we like to combine techniques to get the best results.

Since we've extensively discussed grilling techniques and indirect cooking, we've now naturally arrived at a combination of the two. We call these the "initial sear" and "reverse sear."

The kamado allows for the flexibility to use both techniques in either order. With the Primo Oval, this is possible without rearranging the kamado during cooking. Because of its division, you can grill and cook indirectly at the same time. The Big Green Egg and Kamado Joe both sell a series of half-moon accessories for its larger models that also allow for this way of cooking. These accessories fit in most other models.

Most combination techniques we use demand that we increase or decrease the temperature significantly while cooking. We do this by either placing or removing the heat shield. As mentioned before, a heat shield lowers the dome temperature by about 90°F (50°C). We use this for a number of techniques.

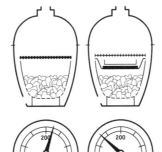

Initial sear

To show how this technique works, let's take a large piece of beef as as an example. The cast-iron grid in this technique is important because we want to grill on medium heat.

- Fire up the kamado with a cast-iron grid in place to 425°F (220°C). Create a single hot spot in the middle of the fire box (in a Primo Oval, directly under the half grid).
- Make sure the grid is hot and grill a nice crust on your steak with the vents in the same position as for other grill techniques (see page 59). Take the meat out of the kamado. Don't worry if it cools off a little.
- Remove the cast-iron grid from the kamado. Make sure to have a place where you can put this without making burn marks.
- Install the heat shield and a drip pan in the kamado with a standard grid. Preferably put sand or salt in the drip pan instead of water. More moisture would prevent a good crust on the meat.
- Put the meat back on the standard grid. Close the vents to almost closed at the top vent and one finger width on the bottom vent. This is to reduce the airflow as much as possible. It can take a while before the temperature drops. Aim for 250 to 280°F (120 to 140°C); that should be doable.
- Use a food thermometer to determine the final internal temperature at which to remove the meat, depending on the recipe and your own preference.
- Because the final cooking is at a relatively low dome temperature, there's no real need to let the meat rest long.

Reverse sear or end sear

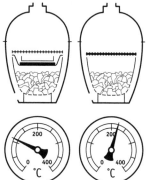

This looks like the reverse procedure of the initial sear, but there are a few other factors that we need to take into account. The ingredient is first cooked almost to the final temperature, then grilled to finish. The thickness of the piece is important when reverse searing. If 130°F (55°C) is the desired internal temperature for a piece of meat, then we stop cooking at 125°F (50°C) for a 2¾-inch (7-cm) prime rib or bone-in rib-eye and start grilling. With thinner pieces, like a domestic duck breast, we'd stop at 120°F (48°C). The heat of the grilling process penetrates quickly to the interior of the meat when the meat is already close to the right temperature.

- Fire up the kamado to 300°F (150°C) and create a single hot spot in the middle of the fire box (in a Primo Oval, directly under the half grid).
- Configure the kamado for slow-cooking with the heat shield and the standard grid (see page 76); pour some water in the drip pan as you only want to grill the crust later.
- Place the meat on the grid and cook with a dome temperature of 212°F (100°C), until it is 10 degrees below the desired final internal temperature.
- Take the food out of the kamado and keep it warm! If you let it cool off, it will not be at the desired temperature for grilling. If you wish, you can wrap it in aluminum foil.
- Now quickly but carefully remove all the loose elements from the kamado and replace them with the cast-iron grid.
- Heat the kamado to 425°F (220°C) and give the grid time to heat up.
- Check to see if you can start grilling by holding your hand briefly above the grid. You should be able to hold it there for no more than 3 seconds.
- Place the food on the hottest area. Grill the meat a few minutes or until it has a nice crust; turn frequently and don't worry about grill marks.

- Use a food thermometer to determine whether it's reached the correct final internal temperature, depending on the recipe and your preference.
- If the internal temperature is about 2 degrees below the desired temperature, your meat can rest off the grill on a warm spot for about 5 minutes. The grilling heat will permeate throughout the meat and you'll lose fewer juices when cutting it.

When to use initial sear and when to use reverse sear?

The advantage of the initial sear combination is that you immediately kill all bacteria on the exterior of your meat. This is important for chicken and pork. It's also the way to avoid the exterior becoming too dark and the interior being too raw. We typically choose initial sear for meat on the bone, so we can keep a close eye on the process with a probe thermometer with a wire. The entire process is orderly and predictable. The downside is that there is often more transition from crust to pink to red meat and that the crust is usually not as pretty as with a reverse sear.

The reverse sear or end sear combination gives a nice crispy crust and an almost uniform doneness down to the core of the meat. The downside, though, is a greater risk for the meat to overcook or stay raw if you start grilling at the wrong moment. Also, a bone can have an unpredictable influence on the cooking process. With grilling, it can block heat or even pass on the heat more quickly. The initial sear might be a better choice in this case.

Choose a reverse sear for ingredients with a thick layer of fat, so you only have to deal with intense grease fumes briefly. It's difficult to lower the temperature in the kamado when you've just literally poured oil on the fire, as it would continue to fume for a long time throughout the cooking process. We also use the reverse sear for pieces that don't suffer too much if you sear them for too long, like the pork neck. Grilling after baking makes for a tastier crust.

You can use both techniques for nearly all grill recipes. For larger pieces of meat with a high fat content it's possible to grill, then slow-cook, and in the end freshen up the crust. We use a bone-in ribeye in the following recipe, which gets both an initial sear and an end sear. This will give you practice with both techniques and changing heat shields and drip pans.

Initial and End Sear of a Bone-In Ribeye or Prime Rib

Initial and End Sear of a Bone-In Ribeye or Prime Rib

With this preparation, we use two combination techniques to get a nice crust and as much flavor as possible in the meat. A flat piece of bone-in meat weighing about 1¾ pounds (800 g) will get the best ratio of crust to red meat. Bone-in ribeye is marbled meat and both its color and flavor will benefit from the initial and end sear procedures. It's important to use pepper only at the very last moment to avoid burning it during grilling.

- Fire up the kamado with the cast-iron grid to 425°F (220°C) and create a hot spot in the middle of the charcoal that is big enough to grill the entire steak.
- While the kamado heats, take the meat out of the fridge. Sprinkle it generously with salt and rub into the meat. Let it sit at room temperature for 30 to 45 minutes.
- Place the meat over the hot spot and grill, turning frequently, for 2 to 3 minutes, until it is nicely browned but not blackened.
- Remove the meat from the kamado and remove the grid.

- Install the heat shield and put an empty or sand-filled drip pan on top. Put the cast-iron grid back. The mass of the meat and heat shield will lower the temperature considerably. Limit the airflow. Try to attain a temperature around 265°F (130°C).
- Put the meat back on the grid and slow-cook it for 10 to 15 minutes, until the internal temperature is about 120°F (50°C).
- Remove the meat and wrap it in aluminum foil to keep it warm. Remove the grid, drip pan, and heat shield. Put the grid back and heat up the kamado to 465°F (240°C).
- Unwrap the meat, return it to the grill, and grill it for a few minutes on each side to get a nice crispy crust. Make sure not to overdo it. A nice serving temperature is about 130°F (53 to 56°C) for light pink. Let it rest for a few minutes and cut it in pencil-thick, diagonal slices. Pepper the slices liberally and season with salt to taste.

SERVES 4

- 1 bone-in ribeye or Prime rib, between 1 ¾ and 2 pounds (800 g and 1 kg)
- Coarse sea salt
- Freshly ground black pepper

WHAT YOU NEED

- Cast-iron grid
- Heat shield
- Drip pan
- Clean sand (optional)
- Food thermometer

TEMPERATURE

- 425/265/465°F (220/130/240°C)

TIP *The taste of a really good piece of meat, like this roast, would only be ruined by a sauce. Herb butter should be enough. Make sure to serve with bread or fluffy potatoes to sop up the juices.*

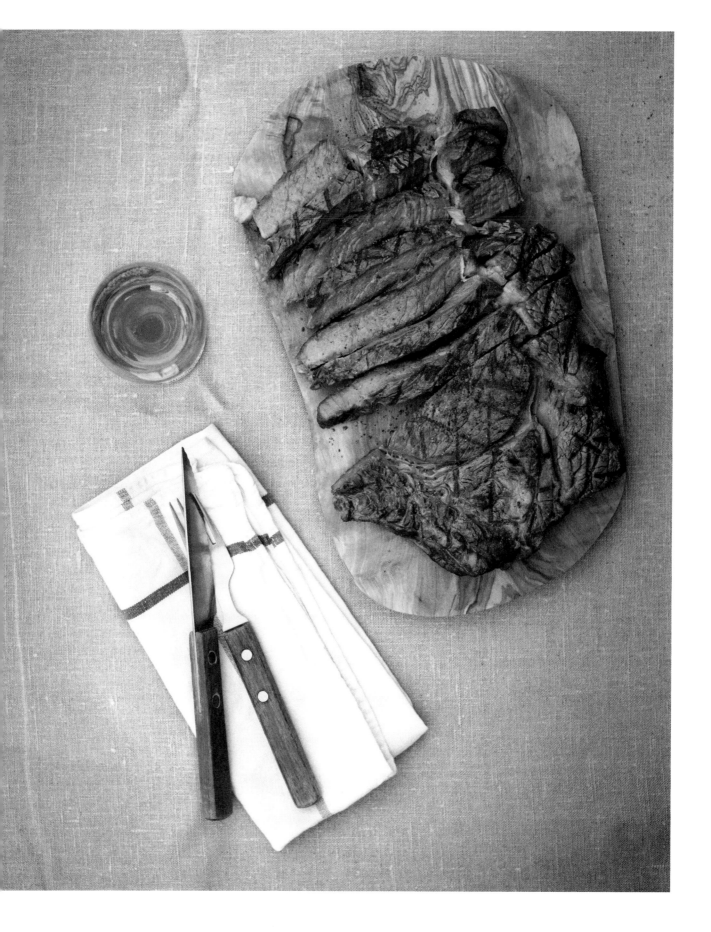

Special techniques

This section of the book is meant for those special techniques that can't be categorized under previously mentioned techniques. We discuss grill planks, roasted vegetables, and "caveman style." At the end of this chapter, we elaborate on one of the most fun techniques to use with the kamado—chicken on a vertical poultry roaster.

Grill planks

We have discussed hot smoking on low temperatures (see page 76). It's usually better to plan to serve warm smoked dishes at the beginning of the menu. It is very hard to get the kamado below 212°F (100°C) once it's been above 390°F (200°C). However, a grill plank is a wonderful solution to get a smoky flavor in an ingredient while direct grilling. Another advantage is that fish fillets that would otherwise quickly fall apart on a grid can be served directly on the plank. The procedure for fish does require a delicate touch, because it can become quite dry.

Cooking on a plank is less gentle than with slow-cooking, because you cook at much higher temperatures with contact heat, steam, and hot air. Plank grilling is not only great for fish, but also for shrimp, poultry fillets, and pork. You can also cook vegetables and mushrooms along with the main ingredient. The entire process generally doesn't take more than 20 minutes since the pieces of food usually don't weigh more than 10½ ounces (300 g).

The planks are often made from cedar or alder wood (a wood traditionally used for fish smoking). Before using, soak the planks for about half an hour in water. Place the ingredient on the soaked plank and position it on a hot grill rack under a dome temperature of 390°F (200°C). The plank will first start to steam, and then you'll get some smoke production—simple and effective. We usually throw out the plank after its first use, but some suppliers claim you can use them multiple times.

Roasting

Roasting in a kamado is the best way to prepare root vegetables. It just takes time. The flavor of the vegetables is surprisingly pure and concentrated, and after roasting, you can do other things with them. Find a spot in the kamado where it's about 390°F (200°C) and there won't be too much direct glow toward the vegetables. We prefer not to use aluminum foil. Our experience is that both potatoes and beets are tastier when their skin has direct contact with the kamado.

These are the most frequently used positions and methods for roasting:

- **On the edge of the fire box while you're grilling.** You need to frequently turn over the vegetables, otherwise they will roast unevenly and may become too dark and have a burned taste. This can happen quickly.
- **On the heat shield while you are baking bread or are doing something else oven-wise.** This is our favorite method. Potatoes roast nicely and become crispy in their skins due to the contact heat of the stone. They are surrounded on all sides by reflected heat.
- **On a grid with indirect techniques.** This is our least favorite method; there is no contact heat and roasting can take so long that the vegetables dry out. With this technique, aluminum foil might be a good idea.

Peeling or leaving the skin on is up to you. If there are black spots on the skin after roasting, we typically peel them, but sometimes potato skin can be very crispy and tasty. After roasting, you can fry both beets and potatoes in a skillet with some oil for extra caramelization; it's delicious. You can do this by first flattening them, but you can also slice or quarter them. We call potatoes prepared this way twice-cooked potatoes. For beets, we usually fry them in slices or quarters and douse them with a little red wine vinegar or balsamic vinegar.

Caveman style

We call all techniques where the ingredients directly touch the charcoal "caveman style." The most common preparation is a thick steak, but it also works very well with vegetables.

For vegetables, we usually blacken the skin and peel or cut it off after cooking. Their core will often acquire a sweet taste. This technique is most known for bell peppers, but leeks, garlic, and onions are also suitable for caveman style. Vegetables placed on charcoal cook in a similar way to when you roast them, but quicker. They will taste smokier and pretty bitter.

What about the steak? Choose a piece of meat that's at least 2 inches (5 cm) thick—there's less risk of overcooking. The principle is comparable to when a person walks over hot coals. The sweat on the foot and the juices in the meat work in similar ways to prevent it from burning immediately, and quickness of action is also important. The gray layer of ash on top of the coals also often keeps heat radiation in check.

- Don't salt the meat beforehand, as we want a layer of steam to surround it before it begins to brown.
- Make a hot spot the size of the meat. Heat up the kamado to about 465°F (240°C).
- Before you put the meat on the coals, fan away the upper layer of ash from the charcoal.
- Place the steak directly on the hot coals, close the dome, and wait at least 4 minutes.
- Turn the meat over and scrape off the coals that stick.
- Wait another 4 minutes.
- Take the meat out of the kamado.
- Let it rest on a cutting board in a warm area for at least 10 minutes.

This last part is very important: Not only to rest the meat itself, but to allow the heat of the crust to penetrate to the interior of the meat. The heat trapped in the outer surface from the coals is so intense, it will finish cooking the meat given enough time. Otherwise, the core might be too red.

It's sometimes hard to determine the right amount of time for this method. Once the meat is on a board, you can stick a thermometer in and watch the internal temperature increase. We are happy with medium-rare, at 125°F (52°C), but you won't hear us complain if it's a bit more rare.

Poultry on a stand or vertical roaster

The poultry that we use with this technique are chicken, guinea fowl, and turkey. Domestic goose and duck require a different approach because they have more fat under their skin. There are several good methods to prepare large poultry in a kamado. You can prepare the bird indirectly on a rack or grid, with a drip pan on the heat shield. This resembles preparing a large piece of meat or roast, without the initial or end sear. Ideally choose a temperature of about 300°F (150°C) and allow it to increase to 355 to 375°F (180 to 190°C) later to get a crispy skin.

The best and least complicated way of roasting a bird is on a chicken stand. This is a variation on the well-known beer-can chicken, in which everyone believes that the beer from the can evaporates. This unfortunately isn't true; there is just as much beer in a can at the end of the process. (There are other reasons why the chicken stays so juicy; more about that later.) The annoying thing is that the can often topples over, so now there is a rack in which you can place the can. Not a bad idea, but it's best just to omit the can.

Then there is a ceramic poultry stand, where you can pour a little liquid into a notch. It works well, but isn't perfect yet. This roaster is available in chicken size and turkey size. Our absolute favorite chicken stand is the most simple and effective one—a metal wire chicken roaster. This is the one we use.

The standard-size poultry stand is suited for chicken and guinea fowl up to 4½ pounds (2 kg) in the regular and medium kamados. We use a larger size stand for turkeys up to about 15 pounds (6.8 kg). Otherwise, its collar will touch the upper wall in most kamados and you risk the turkey toppling over.

Aside from this accessory, you only need a drip pan and a standard grid. Use a firm drip pan with a rim of at least 2 inches (5 cm) and a diameter equal to or slightly larger than the bird you're about to prepare. Good chicken and turkey don't need to be smoked; the roasting process itself should provide enough flavor. Why is this such an effective method? In this case, it's the convection that does the heavy lifting, since the bird is mostly protected from direct glow by the drip pan. There is a lot of Maillard reaction because the bird is heated from all sides. The liquid in the drip pan will immediately begin to evaporate because it's in direct contact with the grid. The steam protects the bird against too much browning in the beginning.

The most important thing is that, because of the shape of the stand, the bird cooks both inside and outside from steam and hot air. What is promised by the beer-can method happens here. The water in the drip pan prevents grease and protein from the drip from smoldering and causing a burnt smell. You can add beer, wine, or liquor to the drip pan for the aroma. Fresh herbs, garlic, and citrus fruits also work well.

It's important to control the evaporation so that when the bird needs another 20 minutes to bake, the drip pan is nearly empty. The reflection of the heat in the dome at the end is crucial for a crispy skin. This is why the bird sits upright; much of the fat is in its collar. The fat will begin to melt and slide downward under the skin over the breast meat and the back. This way you automatically baste the leaner parts during the baking process. When the subcutaneous fat has melted away, the skin becomes crisp and starts to expand away from the meat. This is usually a sign the bird is ready.

- Fire up the kamado to 375°F (190°C) with the chicken stand (for birds below 3½ pounds/1.5 kg). With larger birds, we start at a lower cooking temperature (usually around 300°F/150°C), and during the last 45 minutes we heat it up to 355°F (180°C) for a crispy skin.
- Position the bird on the roaster. It's best to leave the elastic or rope around the legs and wings and only take them away when you start cutting to serve.
- Put the stand with the bird in the drip pan.
- Fill the drip pan halfway with water, to below the legs of the bird.
- Plan on cooking for about 45 minutes for each 2 pounds (1 kg) of bird. Refill the drip pan every half-hour until about 30 minutes before the bird should be finished.
- The bird is ready at an internal temperature of 160°F (70°C) in a leg, or if you can easily pull off a leg. The puffing of the skin is another good indicator that it's ready.
- Allow the bird to rest at room temperature for 5 to 10 minutes before you carve it.

A refresher on the number of hot spots and traveling

As you know by now, hot spots are an important part of using the kamado, so let's review the basics. Sometimes individual hot spots are needed when grilling directly. A hot spot appears where you initially put a fire starter. You mostly grill directly over the hot spot, which can be a single spot or a triangle of three. If they are close enough to each other, everything put in between these patterns on the grid is considered grilling over a hot area. If the ingredient is not cooked fully after getting the right color, it then should be moved outside of this hotter area to cook more slowly.

After you've been grilling for more than half an hour, the hot area on the grid will typically move or expand laterally. The glow will seek out new charcoal or it will follow fat dripping. We call this traveling.

It's better to ignite a small portion of charcoal (i.e., create one or two hot spots) when preparing to smoke or slow-cook. The less charcoal is glowing, the easier it will be to maintain a low temperature. A hot spot is the place to insert smoking wood, as the wood has to be in direct contact with the burning charcoal to start smoking. When slow-cooking a long time, this initial hot spot (or two) will move vertically. It will burn down into the charcoal toward the air inlet.

If you want a higher temperature , as for making bread or pizza, you can use more starter cubes (as many as five). In this case, because of an abundance of oxygen, the glow will expand both vertically and laterally. After you've given it a lot of air, all the charcoal will burn in an almost uniform layer of heat.

LEFT TO RIGHT:
CERAMIC CHICKEN STAND,
WIRE CHICKEN STAND, WIRE
TURKEY STAND WITH DRIP PAN.

Cedar-Planked Cod

Cod is difficult to grill because of its tendency to fall apart once it's done. This risk doesn't exist with a grill plank. Because of the smoke and steam coming off the plank, the cod sears evenly and attains a definite, but not too bitter, smoky flavor.

· Soak the planks for 30 minutes in water. Fire up the kamado with the cast-iron grid to 425°F (220°C) and create a hot spot large enough (about 3 cubes) for the wood.
· Season the fillets with salt and pepper.
· Place the fillets skin-side down on the planks and position the planks on the grid in the kamado. Close the lid and let them cook for 15 to 20 minutes. The planks will steam for the first 8 minutes, then begin to smolder, and then smoke will develop. The fish will be smoked during the last 7 minutes.

· The plank can warp because of the heat, but that won't affect the outcome. The fish is done once it has reached an internal temperature of 120°F (50°C) or higher.
· Take the planks off the grid with gloves or strong tongs. Lift the fish off the planks with a spatula, sliding it between the flesh and skin to easily remove the skin.

TIP *Place halved chanterelles on top of the fillets and let them smoke alongside the fish. The mushrooms will impart a subtle flavor to the fish.*

SERVES 4

· 4 (5 3/4-ounce/160-g) cod fillets, preferably skin-on
· Coarse sea salt
· Freshly ground black pepper

WHAT YOU NEED

· 2 (6-by-12-inch/15-by-30-cm) cedar wood planks
· Cast-iron grid

TEMPERATURE

· 425°F (220°C)

Cedar-Planked Cod

Roasted Root Vegetables

Roasted Root Vegetables

In this recipe, we like to use three different kinds of beets: golden beets, Chioggia, and the standard purple beets. They each have a different taste, but also a slightly different preparation time. The larger ones might need at least 90 minutes, while for the smaller ones an hour will do. The difference in taste is mostly because of the different amounts of sugar they contain.

For potatoes, we choose a starchy sort. Bintje, Malta, or something like Idaho are ideal. Aside from those, we often use purple potatoes or Andean Sunrise potatoes. Because they are starchy, they have a light texture. They taste different from the boiled potatoes we're used to. Yukon gold potatoes don't work as well here. They remain hard and ultimately dehydrate. A shame! If you only have Yukon potatoes, it's best to pre-boil them for 5 to 10 minutes in ample water before roasting them.

- Fire up the kamado with the heat shield to 425°F (220°C).
- Rinse the dirt off the potatoes and beets. Make a ½-inch (1-cm) incision in each of the potatoes so they won't explode when they are cooking.
- Place the large beets on the heat shield first; 15 minutes later, add the potatoes and other beets so they are done at about the same time. Close the lid and roast the vegetables. Turn the vegetables over every 10 minutes or so, so their skins get crispy but don't burn.
- About an hour after you've put the potatoes on the heat shield, check if they're ready. You can do this by pushing your thumb down on their skin. If the imprint remains, they are ready. Their internal temperature should be about 200°F (90°C). The beets will remain a bit more firm.
- Halve the potatoes and season them with salt and pepper. Quarter the beets and season them with salt and pepper as well.

SERVES 4

- 4 baking potatoes
- 8 beets, different varieties, sizes, and colors
- Coarse sea salt
- Freshly ground black pepper

WHAT YOU NEED
- Heat shield

TEMPERATURE
- 425°F (220°C)

TIP *Mix ¼ cup (55 g) cream cheese, ¼ cup (60 g) mayonnaise, and a handful of finely chopped fresh herbs like parsley and chives and season with salt to taste. Serve this sauce with the root vegetables.*

Caveman-Style Tomahawk Steak

The tomahawk is a large steak with a robust bone. The thickness makes it perfect to prepare directly on the charcoal.

· Take the steak out of the fridge an hour before cooking. In this case, don't dab the meat dry and don't sprinkle it with salt.

· Fire up the kamado without accessories to 460°F (240°C) and create a single, large hot spot.

· Just before you start, wave a piece of cardboard or a newspaper above the charcoal to blow away the loose white ashes.

· Place the steak directly on the charcoal, on its hottest spot.

· Close the lid and wait for about 6 minutes.

· Turn the steak and remove any pieces of coal that have stuck to it.

· Close the lid and wait 3 minutes.

· Take the steak out of the kamado, put it on a platter in a warm area (without foil), and let it rest for about 10 minutes.

· While you wait, place the cast-iron grid in the kamado.

· Check the internal temperature of the steak: A nice serving temperature is 125 to 130°F (50 to 54°C) for rare. Cut the steak into slices of ½ inch (1 cm) thick, sprinkle with coarse salt, and grind a little pepper over them. If the meat is too red (and this happened to us, too), grill the slices, cut-side down, briefly on the grid.

TIP *The smoky, lightly burned flavor and taste of this meat calls for a spicy sauce.*

SERVES 4

· 2 (1 ¼-pound/570-g) bone-in ribeye (or "cowboy") steaks or 1 (3-pound/1.5-kg) tomahawk steak
· Coarse sea salt
· Freshly ground black pepper

WHAT YOU NEED

· Cast-iron grid
· Food thermometer

TEMPERATURE

· 460°F (240°C)

Caveman-Style Tomahawk Steak

PREPARATION TECHNIQUES CHAPTER 5

Chicken on a Poultry Stand

Chicken on a Poutry Stand

We recommend an organic, corn-fed, free-range chicken with a minimal life span of eighty days. In the Netherlands we use yellow-skinned *Kemper Landhoen*, or a *French Label Rouge Poulet Jaune*, but you can use any small-pastured free-range chicken. Yellow-skinned chickens are better suited for the grill than white-skinned. They have more subcutaneous fat because of their diets, and firmer, less-refined meat than white-skinned chickens. You can prepare white-skinned chickens this way, but they are better suited for lower-temperature methods.

· If the chicken is bound with twine or heat-resistant elastic, don't remove it, as it's better for a more even cooking process. If it's not bound, then you can do it yourself later on.

· Rub the chicken all over with the lemon, squeezing as you do. (Keep the squeezed-out lemon parts). Strip the thyme leaves, reserving the stems. Finely chop the thyme leaves and garlic together and place in a small bowl; stir in the oil and salt and add pepper to taste. Rub the chicken skin generously with the herb-garlic oil. Fill the cavity of the chicken with the thyme stems and the squeezed-out lemon quarters. The chicken will gain flavor from inside as well.

· Fire up the kamado with the standard grid to 360°F (180°C).

· Place the chicken on the roaster, bind the legs (if this hasn't been done already) with butcher's twine and a simple knot, and put the roaster in the roasting pan. Fill the roasting pan with water until just beneath the bird's legs. If desired, you may replace a quarter of the water with wine or beer.

· Place the roasting pan on the grid, close the dome, and bake the chicken for about 1 hour (or 45 minutes for every 2 pounds/1 kg), until the meat in a leg has reached at least 160°F (70°C)—it could be as high as 175°F (80°C). Make sure when you measure not to measure at the bone. There are a number of things that indicate whether a chicken is ready: when you can easily move the legs back and forth, and when the skin begins to puff up and comes away from the meat.

· Allow the bird to rest at room temperature for 5 to 10 minutes before you carve it.

SERVES 4

· 1 (2 1/2- to 3-pound/1.2- to 1.4-kg) chicken
· 1 lemon, quartered
· 1 bunch fresh thyme
· 2 cloves garlic, peeled
· About 3 1/2 ounces (100 ml) sunflower oil
· 1 1/2 teaspoons coarse sea salt
· Freshly ground black pepper
· Wine or beer (optional)

WHAT YOU NEED

· Standard grid
· Vertical poultry roaster
· Butcher's twine (if necessary)
· Drip pan
· Food thermometer

TEMPERATURE

· 360°F (180°C)

CHAPTER 6
RECIPES

Now that you've learned the thirteen techniques for cooking with your kamado, you can move on to more advanced recipes. The dishes in this chapter require more patience and more time—and some even combine multiple techniques from the previous chapter. These recipes may look intimidating at first, but after mastering the basics from Chapter 5 you'll have no problem tackling them.

Double-Grilled Flank Steak

A flank steak or flap meat is a beef cut from the stomach muscle, perfectly suited for grilling. As long as it has the right marbling, that is; it needs to have a good amount of intramuscular fat. On the grill, this fat will melt and give the meat flavor and tenderness. Flank steaks don't usually have a layer of fat on the outside, so you can keep grilling without having to worry about billowing thick, white smoke.

This is a cut of work meat, a muscle that during the cow's life saw a lot of action. Therefore it will be less tender than strip steak, so it's not a bad idea to use a marinade. This recipe gives you the option of grilling it plain or using the marinade. When serving, it's very important to cut thin slices against the grain. It's very easy to determine the direction of the grain in a flank steak. It's more or less a half-moon of meat strips.

You can serve this as a main course or use it for steak strips in a salad or wrap.

· Make the marinade (if using): Mix the onion, sweet peppers, garlic, jalapeño, cilantro, lime juice, oil, and cumin in a shallow pan and then rub the flank steak with the mixture. Let it marinate in the fridge for 4 hours.

· Fire up the kamado with the cast-iron grid to 450°F (230°C). Create a triangle of three hot spots broad enough to grill the entire flap of meat.

· Grill the beef: Take the flank steak out of the fridge (if you marinated it, take the beef out and keep the marinade for later use; see Tip below) and dab it dry. Sprinkle it with salt and thoroughly rub it in.

· Put the meat on the grid over the hot spots and grill it for 4 minutes on each side, making nice grill marks. Close the lid after each action.

· Take the flank steak out of the kamado and place it on a cutting board. Because the meat tapers off at the edges, you can most likely immediately cut and serve those parts. A nice internal temperature is between 127 and 132°F (53 and 56°C), depending on the cut. The thin part will be done slightly earlier.

· The middle part will probably still be red. Cut two or three thick strips from the center piece and put these back on the grill. Cook only the red sides and turn the strips over after 1 minute.

· Briefly let the meat rest on the cutting board and cut it perpendicular to the grain, into strips about ¼ inch (6 mm) wide. Generously season them with pepper and sprinkle with salt.

SERVES 4

FOR THE MARINADE (OPTIONAL)
· 1 red onion, coarsely chopped
· 2 pointed sweet peppers, seeded and coarsely chopped
· 3 cloves garlic, minced
· 1 jalapeño, seeded and cut into rings
· ½ bunch fresh cilantro, leaves chopped
· Juice of 3 limes
· About 3 tablespoons olive oil, about the same amount as the lime juice
· Pinch of ground cumin

FOR THE BEEF
· 1 (2-pound/1-kg) flank steak (flap meat)
· Coarse sea salt
· Freshly ground black pepper

WHAT YOU NEED
· Cast-iron grid
· Food thermometer

TEMPERATURE
· 450°F (230°C)

TIP *If you used marinade, briefly bring it to a boil and serve with the meat as a warm dressing.*

Grilled Salad Greens with Balsamic Dressing

This mildly sour dressing goes perfectly with the slight bitterness of the various salad greens. The Little Gem will caramelize before getting too bitter. The radicchio can be somewhat overpowering, so use it in moderation. We tried this out with a number of different compact leaf greens and found it also works especially well on Chinese cabbage—and, of course, onions.

· Make the dressing: Pour the vinegar into a bowl and add the sugar. Mix with a hand blender while slowly pouring in the oil. Season the dressing with some salt and pepper to taste.
· Make the salad: Fire up the kamado with the cast-iron grid to 390°F (200°C) and create a triangle of hot spots.

· Halve the vegetables lengthwise. Place them on the grill cut-sides down and cook for 2 minutes. Rotate them 90 degrees and cook for another 2 minutes. Close the lid after each action.
· Occasionally take a look at the grilling surface: The greens should roast without getting burned. If they turn out to be a little too blackened on the outside, simply peel away the outermost layers.
· Arrange the vegetables on a platter and lightly sprinkle them with the dressing.

TIP *You can sprinkle the grilled vegetables with some shredded buffalo mozzarella and toasted pine nuts.*

SERVES 4 AS A SIDE DISH

FOR THE DRESSING
· About 3 1/2 ounces (100 ml) balsamic vinegar
· 1 tablespoon granulated sugar
· About 7 ounces (200 ml) sunflower oil
· Sea salt
· Freshly ground black pepper

FOR THE SALAD
· 2 heads radicchio
· 4 heads Belgian endive
· 4 heads Little Gem lettuce

WHAT YOU NEED
· Cast-iron grid
· Hand blender or whisk

TEMPERATURE
· 390°F (200°C)

Bay Leaf-Grilled Quail

A rub is nothing more than a spice mix used for flavoring meat, fish, or poultry. We encourage you to experiment with various spices and herbs until you have developed some favorite rubs of your own. We developed this preparation for smaller kamados without a heat shield—first with partridge, and later with quail— because they are basically the only birds you can grill in a small kamado. The bay leaves were an educated guess on how to shield these little birds from the heat while they were cooking through, without burning them. The bay leaves give a pleasant aroma without overpowering the rub.

· Make the rub: In a baking dish, combine the parsley, oil, garlic, salt, and some pepper to taste. Rub the quails with the mixture. Place them in the dish, cover, and refrigerate for a couple of hours.

· Make the quail: Fire up the kamado with the cast-iron grid to 390°F (200°C) and create a triangle of hot spots.

· Remove the quail from the marinade and put them on the grid breast-side down. Grill over a hot spot for 3 minutes. Place 3 bay leaves on the cooler part of the grid in an overlapping "roof tile" pattern with a quail on top. Repeat with the rest of the bay leaves and quails and cook them for another 6 to 8 minutes. Cover the grill after each action. The bay leaves will impart a wonderful aroma to the quails while also making sure they won't burn.

· Remove the quails when the internal temperature of the breast reaches about 160°F (70°C).

· Serve whole as a starter or several quail as an entire meal. We like to eat them with grilled leaf greens.

SERVES 4 AS A STARTER

FOR THE RUB
· 1 bunch fresh flat-leaf parsley, leaves minced
· 1/4 cup (60 ml) sunflower oil
· 3 cloves garlic, minced
· 2 level tablespoons coarse sea salt or kosher salt
· Freshly ground black pepper

FOR THE QUAIL
· 4 whole quails, heads and innards removed
· 12 fresh bay leaves

WHAT YOU NEED
· Cast-iron grid
· Food thermometer

TEMPERATURE
· 390°F (200°C)

Squid with Aioli

You can buy these squid either frozen and cleaned or fresh (we explain how to clean them yourself below). We love these grilled and cut into rings as a side dish with a glass of white wine. Just one bite transports us straight to the Mediterranean.

· Make the aioli: Put the garlic in a food processor with the parsley, wine, lemon juice, and ginger syrup and blend until smooth. In a medium bowl, mix together the sour cream and mayonnaise. Spoon in the garlic-parsley mixture. Season with salt and pepper to taste. Cover and refrigerate until needed. The aioli will keep in the refrigerator for 3 to 5 days.
· Clean the squid: Cut out the beak in the middle of all the tentacles. Place your finger behind the head and pull the cartilage from the body. If you do this correctly, you also pull out the intestines. Rinse the body and the tentacles under running water.

· Fire up the kamado with the cast-iron grid to 390°F (200°C). Use a broad grilling surface made out of three hot spots.
· Grill the squid for 2 minutes on each side (you can rotate after 1 minute for a nice grill mark). Close the lid after each action.
· The squid are done when firm to the touch, but not dry.
· Cut the squid into rings or serve whole with the aioli.

TIP *If you prefer a less pronounced garlic flavor, you could blanch the cloves for several minutes in boiling water before pureeing them.*

SERVES 4 AS A STARTER OR TAPAS

· 8 fresh squids

FOR THE AIOLI

· 2 large cloves garlic, peeled
· 1/2 bunch fresh flat-leaf parsley, stemmed and chopped
· 2 teaspoons white wine
· 2 teaspoons fresh lemon juice
· 2 teaspoons ginger syrup (from a jar of ginger)
· 2 tablespoons sour cream
· 1/2 cup (100 g) mayonnaise
· Sea salt
· Freshly ground black pepper

WHAT YOU NEED

· Cast-iron grid

TEMPERATURE

· 390°F (200°C)

Vegetable Lasagna

Who doesn't love lasagna? With melted cheese, tomato sauce, and fresh vegetables, it's difficult to mess up—but you can make it even better with the kamado. The grill imparts a smoky flavor to the lasagna that really takes this Italian classic up a notch.

· Make the tomato sauce: In a sauté pan, heat the oil over medium-high heat. Sauté the onion and celery with the rosemary, thyme, and sage until the onion is translucent, lowering the heat to medium if necessary, about 8 minutes. Add the garlic and sauté for another minute. Add the tomatoes, mix, and let them simmer for 15 minutes. Puree the sauce with a hand blender and allow it to boil down until it is thicker. Season it with salt and pepper to taste. Set aside to cool.

· Make the lasagna: Grind some fresh pepper over the tomatoes and set them aside. Layer the eggplant and zucchini in the baking dish, salting each layer. Cover the dish with aluminum foil and allow it to rest for half an hour. The vegetables will release a lot of moisture, which is what we're looking for. Lift the vegetables from the dish, rub off the salt, and dab the vegetables dry with a paper towel.

· Fire up the kamado with the cast-iron grid to 390°F (200°C).

Make a broad grill surface out of three hot spots.

· Grill the eggplant and zucchini slices for 2 to 3 minutes on each side, until they are browned and crispy. Close the lid after each action.

· Remove the grilled vegetables to a cutting board to cool off. Take the grid out of the kamado and install the heat shield. Put the grid back. Bring the temperature back to 390°F (200°C).

· Place a layer of eggplant slices on the bottom of a small baking dish and scoop a thin layer of sauce on top. Cover them with a layer of zucchini slices, sprinkle on some cheese, and cover with tomato slices. Repeat until you've used all the vegetables and finish with a layer of cheese.

· Place the dish on the grid, close the lid, and bake for 40 to 45 minutes, until the top is golden brown.

· Let it sit for 10 to 15 minutes before serving.

TIP *Serve the lasagna with a fresh green salad and fresh bread, like the focaccia on page 130.*

SERVES 3 OR 4 AS A MAIN COURSE OR 6 AS A STARTER

FOR THE TOMATO SAUCE
· 3 tablespoons olive oil classico
· 1 white onion, coarsely chopped
· 1 celery stalk, coarsely chopped
· 1 tablespoon fresh rosemary needles
· 2 teaspoons fresh thyme leaves
· 5 small fresh sage leaves
· 3 garlic cloves, minced
· 6 Roma tomatoes, coarsely chopped
· About 3/4 teaspoon sea salt
· Freshly ground black pepper

FOR THE LASAGNA
· Freshly ground black pepper
· 2 medium beefsteak tomatoes, thickly sliced
· 2 medium globe eggplants, thickly sliced lengthwise
· 2 medium zucchini, thickly sliced lengthwise
· 2 tablespoons kosher salt
· 1 1/3 cups (150 g) grated aged cheese, such as Parmigiano-Reggiano

WHAT YOU NEED
· Hand blender
· Cast-iron grid
· Heat shield
· A baking dish that will fit in your kamado, about 6 by 12 inches (15 by 30 cm)

TEMPERATURE
· 390°F (200°C)

Beech-Smoked Mackerel

Mackerel is a fatty fish with which you can hardly go wrong. Whether you cook it at a high temperature (indirect), on a grilling plank, or with hot smoke, mackerel usually comes out fine. Most types of mackerel are at their best during the summer. The beech wood gives the fish a mild smoke flavor.

· Fire up the kamado with a single hot spot to 300°F (150°C).
· Put a handful of smoking chips or one chunk directly on top of the charcoal hot spot. Now put the heat shield and the standard grid in place. The drip pan is optional, because whole mackerels don't release a lot of moisture and fat compared to fillets.
· Put the mackerels on the grid, close the lid, and let the temperature rise to a maximum of 250°F (120°C) during the smoking.

· After about 20 minutes, check whether the mackerels are done: To do this, stick one with a knife until you hit the vertebrae, making sure enough of the meat is visible that you can judge its tenderness. Tender mackerel loses its translucence and the meat becomes flaky. The internal temperature should be about 120°F (50°C).

TIP *You can make a mackerel mayonnaise that is great spread on a piece of toast or a slice of dark bread. Fillet the mackerels. Carefully check that you have removed all the bones. Break up the fillets in a bowl with a spoon. Add several tablespoons mayonnaise, 1 tablespoon finely chopped parsley, and the juice of ½ lemon for each mackerel. Season with a pinch of salt and pepper to taste.*

SERVES 4

· 4 whole mackerels, cleaned
· Coarse salt
· Freshly ground black pepper

WHAT YOU NEED
· Beech smoking wood (chips or a chunk)
· Heat shield
· Standard grid
· Drip pan (optional)

TEMPERATURE
· 250°F (120°C)

Cherry-Smoked Venison

At our restaurant, Pure Passie, we work closely with a hunter who is very active in sustainable wildlife management in the Hoge Veluwe National Park in the Netherlands. During deer season, he occasionally brings us a deer that we then clean and dress ourselves. We love this pure organic meat. We also find it important to process the entire animal. Nothing goes to waste. The fillets are perfect for brining and smoking on the kamado.

· Crush the juniper berries and peppercorns in a mortar. In a large pot, combine 5 cups (1.2 L) water, the crushed juniper and peppercorns, the garlic, rosemary, thyme, salt, brown sugar, and bay leaf. Bring them to a boil, then remove from the heat and let cool.
· Strain the cooled brine water. Place the venison fillet in a sealable container and pour the brine over it, making sure the fillet is completely submerged. Seal the container and refrigerate for at least 24 hours.

· Take the fillet out of the brine and dab it dry with paper towels. Discard the brine.
· Fire up the kamado with a single hot spot to about 225°F (110°C).
· Put a handful of smoking chips over the hot spot or place two chunks on top of it. Now place the heat shield, the drip pan with a layer of water, and the grid.
· Put the fillet on the grid.
· Close the dome and wait until the temperature has reached a stable 175°F (80°C). Smoke the venison for about 30 minutes, until the meat has an internal temperature of 115°F (47°C), giving it a bright red color.
· Cut the fillet into thin slices and serve as a carpaccio.

TIP *You can garnish the venison with slices of balsamic-marinated baby portobellos or mango chutney.*

SERVES 4 AS A STARTER

· 10 juniper berries
· 4 peppercorns
· 4 cloves garlic, thinly sliced
· 2 sprigs fresh rosemary, leaves chopped
· 2 sprigs fresh thyme, leaves chopped
· About 1/2 cup (100 g) sea salt
· 1/4 cup (50 g) light brown sugar
· 1 fresh bay leaf
· About 1 pound (500 g) venison fillet, membranes removed

WHAT YOU NEED

· Cherry smoking wood (chips or chunks)
· Heat shield
· Drip pan
· Standard grid
· Food thermometer

TEMPERATURE

· 175°F (80°C)

Technique: hot smoking
and slow-cooking

Oak- and Apple-Smoked Pork Belly

Brining pork belly before you smoke it will make it even tastier. When you brine the pork for a full 72 hours, the salt solution and flavor molecules will reach all the way to the core of the meat. This also helps the pork retain its beautiful color.

Smoking contributes a lot as well. The oak provides the deep color and the robust smoke flavor. The apple wood and the maple syrup give the smoked pork belly a softer, mildly sweet taste.

· Make the brine: Crush the juniper berries in a mortar. In a large bowl, combine the hot water with the crushed juniper, the garlic, salt, brown sugar, and bay leaf so that the sugar and salt dissolve. Add the cold water and allow the brine to cool down.

· Place the pork in the brine, cover it, and refrigerate for at least 72 hours.

· Take the pork out of the brine and dab it dry with paper towels. Discard the brine.

· Fire up the kamado with a single hot spot to about 225°F (110°C).

· Place the oak chunks on top of the charcoal first, then the apple wood. Place the heat shield, fill the drip pan with a layer of water, and then install the standard grid.

· Put the pork on the grid, close the dome, and control the kamado with the top vent until it has returned to about 225°F (110°C).

· Smoke the pork belly for 3 to 5 hours; the timing will depend on the thickness of the meat—insert a probe thermometer to check the internal temperature after about 2 hours.

· After about 2 hours, the water will have evaporated. There is no need to add more.

· Brush the pork with the maple syrup about 30 minutes before serving, when the internal temperature is about 140°F (60°C).

· Remove the pork when the internal temperature reaches about 160°F (70°C).

· Transfer the pork to a cutting board and thinly slice it.

TIP *Smoked pork belly isn't just tasty when it's warm. If you cool it down within the hour, it will keep for at least 5 more days in the fridge. If you thinly slice the cold pork, you can eat it with some coarse mustard and honey. It's also delicious on fresh baked bread.*

SERVES 6 TO 8 AS A STARTER, COLD CUT, OR SNACK

FOR THE BRINE
· 4 juniper berries
· 2 cups (480 ml) hot water
· 2 cloves garlic, halved
· About 1/2 cup (100 g) sea salt
· 1/4 cup (50 g) light brown sugar
· 1 fresh bay leaf
· 3 cups (720 ml) cold water

FOR THE PORK BELLY
· About 2 pounds (1 kg) pork belly, no skin
· 2 1/2 ounces (75 ml) maple syrup

WHAT YOU NEED
· 2 large chunks oak wood and 2 chunks apple wood
· Heat shield
· Drip pan
· Standard grid
· Silicone brush

TEMPERATURE
· 225°F (110°C)

Focaccia

When you are making focaccia, there is an infinite amount of possible flavors. Sprinkle it with some sea salt and finely chopped rosemary. Or fill the dough, before folding it over, with finely sliced sun-dried tomatoes, grated cheese, olives, or herbs. A sweet filling is also delicious—think figs, apricots, or raisins. Let your imagination run wild!

· In a stand mixer fitted with a dough hook, combine the flours, salt, yeast, lemon juice, and ½ cup (120 ml) of the water. Mix them into a smooth, cohesive dough. Add another 1 tablespoon water once the dough is thoroughly combined. At the very last moment, pour the oil into the mixing bowl and mix to incorporate it. Check with a food thermometer that the dough has a temperature of 77°F (25°C); otherwise it won't properly rise. If it is lower, keep on kneading a little longer.

· Grease the springform or pizza pan with extra oil.

· On a lightly floured countertop, flatten the dough and fold the edges back in. Brush it with oil. Now turn the dough over so that the folds are facedown; brush this side with oil as well. Place the dough in the pan and allow it to rise at warm room temperature for 2 hours. Each half hour, thoroughly press down on the dough, making sure it is evenly distributed throughout the pan by the end.

· Fire up the kamado to 425°F (220°C).

· Install the heat shield, put the grid into place, put the pizza stone on top, and then wait until it has come back to 425°F (220°C).

· Grease your fingertips with some oil and form small dimples in the focaccia dough. Add any toppings you like. Place the pan on the stone (or the deep dish on the grid), close the kamado, and bake until the focaccia is golden brown, about 25 minutes.

· Remove the pan to a wire rack and unmold the dough.

MAKES 1 FOCACCIA

· 10 tablespoons (100 g) durum (semolina) flour
· 3/4 cup plus 1 tablespoon (100 g) wheat flour
· 1 1/2 cups (200 g) all-purpose flour, plus more for dusting
· 1 1/2 teaspoons kosher salt or coarse salt
· 1 teaspoon dry yeast
· 1 teaspoon fresh lemon juice
· 1/2 cup (120 ml) plus 1 tablespoon warm water (110 to 115°F/43 to 46°C)
· 1 teaspoon olive oil, plus more for greasing

WHAT YOU NEED
· Food thermometer
· 12-inch (30-cm) springform or deep-dish pizza pan
· Heat shield
· Standard grid
· Pizza stone

TEMPERATURE
· 425°F (220°C)

Whole-Wheat Spelt Bread

Kneading is very important when baking bread. Only when the gluten has been sufficiently activated is the dough ready to bake. You can check this by slowly pulling at a small piece of dough. Activated gluten will give the dough the necessary elasticity to form a nice thin sheet. If your dough sheet tears when you pull it apart, it means you will have to keep kneading a little longer.

· In a stand mixer fitted with a dough hook, combine the flour, salt, yeast, and water. Mix them into a smooth, cohesive dough. Pour in the oil and mix to incorporate it. Check with a food thermometer that the dough has reached 77°F (25°C); otherwise, it won't properly rise. If it is lower, continue kneading a little longer.

· Place the dough on a countertop, on top of a clean, flour-dusted dishcloth. Place a second clean flour-dusted dishcloth over the dough (flour-side down), then cover it all with plastic wrap. Let the dough rise for 1 to 2 hours, until doubled in size.

· Flatten the dough and form it into a ball by tucking under the edges with both hands. Cover with a damp towel and let it rise for another 1 to 2 hours.

· Place the dough, seam facing up, on a flour-dusted work surface and press it into a thin square. Fold the edges toward the center of the dough. Turn the dough over and shape it into a compact ball.

· Sprinkle the pumpkin seeds over a plate and brush the dough lightly with water. Roll the dough through the pumpkin seeds and put it seam-side down on a flour-dusted dishcloth. Let it rise for another 45 minutes.

· Fire up the kamado to 410°F (210°C). Install the heat shield and grid, and put the pizza stone on top. Close the lid and let the kamado come back to 410°F (210°C).

· Dust the pizza stone with the cornmeal and place the dough, seam down, on the stone. Close the kamado and bake until the crust is crisp, approximately 40 minutes.

· Remove the bread to a wire rack to cool.

TIP *It's very easy to make a tasty variation on this bread by mixing the dough with 1/3 cup (40 g) coarsely chopped toasted hazelnuts and 1/3 cup (40 g) toasted chopped walnuts. Make sure you do this only after you have added the oil.*

MAKES 1 LOAF OF BREAD

· About 3 1/3 cups (400 g) whole wheat spelt flour, plus more for dusting
· 2 teaspoons fine sea salt
· 3/4 teaspoon dry yeast
· 1 cup plus 1 tablespoon (260 ml) warm water (110 to 115°F/43 to 46°C)
· 1 teaspoon olive oil
· About 1/4 cup (25 g) pepitas (hulled pumpkin seeds)
· 2 tablespoons coarse cornmeal

WHAT YOU NEED

· Food thermometer
· Heat shield
· Standard grid
· Pizza stone

TEMPERATURE

· 410°F (210°C)

Technique: baking

Quiche

You can improvise endlessly with the fillings for quiche, but these are two of our favorites. More robust vegetables like broccoli or cauliflower are best sliced to ensure tenderness. The amount of custard needed to bind everything together depends on the ingredients and the size of the pie. Make sure all ingredients are completely covered by custard.

Vegetarian Filling

1 tablespoon olive oil • 2 white onions, thinly sliced • 2 cloves garlic, crushed • 1½ pounds (680 g) mixed mushrooms, such as baby portobello, shiitake, and oyster, sliced or chopped • 3 medium tomatoes, thinly sliced

Broccoli-Salmon Filling

1 tablespoon olive oil • 7 ounces (200 g) leeks, sliced into thin rings • 10½ ounces (300 g) broccoli florets, sliced • About 1 pound (455 g) smoked salmon trimmings

· Make the crust: In a stand mixer fitted with a dough hook, combine the flour, butter, salt, egg, and water. Mix until you get a smooth, cohesive dough. Wrap the dough in plastic wrap and set it aside in the refrigerator for 30 minutes.

· Make the custard: In a medium bowl, combine the cream, milk, egg yolks, and eggs. Season with salt and pepper and beat with a mixer.

· Make the filling: Prepare the ingredients for the filling of your choice: Heat the oil in a sauté pan and stir in the vegetables until tender. Season with salt and pepper.

· Fit a sheet of parchment paper on the bottom of the springform pan. Clamp the sides around the base and cut off the excess paper with a pair of scissors.

· Fire up the kamado with the heat shield, grid, and pizza stone in place to 390°F (200°C).

· Remove the dough from the fridge. Lightly dust a work surface with flour and roll out the dough until it's about ¼ inch (6 mm) thick. Using the springform base as a template, cut out a dough circle and use it to line the pan.

· Roll out the dough again and cut out a long, straight strip 1½ to 2 inches (4 to 5 cm) wide and use that to line the walls of the pan, pinching it together with the base.

· Poke the dough bottom with a fork. Evenly spread the cooked filling ingredients over the bottom. For the vegetarian filling, arrange the tomatoes over the cooked ingredients; for the broccoli-salmon filling, scatter the salmon over the cooked ingredients. Stir the custard and pour over the filling.

· Place the pan on top of the pizza stone, close the dome, and bake the quiche until the top is golden brown and the custard is set, about 1 hour.

· Remove the pan to a wire rack. Unlatch the sides and take off the pan. Let the quiche cool for a few minutes before serving it.

MAKES ONE 9-INCH QUICHE

FOR THE CRUST
- 2 ¾ cups (360 g) all-purpose flour, plus more for dusting
- ¼ cup (1/2 stick/60 g) cold unsalted butter, diced
- 1 teaspoon sea salt
- 1 egg
- ½ cup (120 ml) cold water

FOR THE CUSTARD
- ¾ cup plus 1 tablespoon (200 ml) heavy cream
- ½ cup (120 ml) milk
- 5 egg yolks
- 2 eggs
- 1 teaspoon coarse salt
- Freshly ground black pepper

VARIABLE
- Filling of your choice

WHAT YOU NEED
- Hand blender
- 9-inch (23-cm) springform pan
- Heat shield
- Standard grid
- Pizza stone

TEMPERATURE
- 390°F (200°C)

TIP *Preparing the dough really isn't that much work, but if you feel like whipping up your kamado quiche even faster, you can always work with store-bought pastry dough.*

Technique: baking

Apple-Almond Crumble Cake

With their crispy sweet-and-sour taste, Jonagold or Dutch Elstar apples are just perfect for this crumble cake. If you can't find these, use either Fuji or Pink Lady apples. To make things a little more interesting, we also decided to use coarse sea salt. Because you can taste the individual coarse grains, you will get a different taste sensation with every bite.

· Make the dough: Using a stand mixer fitted with the paddle attachment, combine the flour, sugar, butter, egg, egg yolks, and salt. Mix until they form a smooth, cohesive dough. Wrap in plastic wrap and refrigerate for 30 minutes.
· Fit a sheet of parchment paper on the bottom of the springform pan. Clamp the sides around the base and cut off the excess paper with a pair of scissors.
· Fire up the kamado with the heat shield, grid, and pizza stone in place to 355°F (180°C).
· Remove the dough from the fridge. Lightly dust a work surface with flour and roll out the dough until it's about ¼ inch (6 mm) thick. Using the springform base as a template, cut out a dough circle and line the bottom of the pan.
· Roll out the dough again and cut out a long, straight strip 1½ to 2 inches (4 to 5 cm) wide and use

that to line the walls of the pan, pinching it together with the base.
· Make the filling: In a medium bowl, stir together the apples, raisins, and cinnamon. Spread them over the crust.
· Make the almond mixture: In a medium bowl, combine the butter, flour, granulated sugar, and vanilla sugar. One by one, add the eggs while stirring continuously. Stir in the rum. Spread the mixture over the apples.
· Make the crumble: In a clean bowl, using your fingers, combine the butter, sugar, both flours, and the salt until you have a nice crumbly dough. Sprinkle it over the filling. Cover the surface completely; you might not need all of the crumble mixture.
· Place the springform pan on top of the pizza stone, close the dome, and bake until the top is golden brown and a skewer inserted in the cake near the center comes out mostly clean, 60 to 70 minutes.
· Remove the pan to a wire rack. Unlatch the sides and take off the pan. Let the cake cool on the rack before serving it.

TIP *Keep scraped vanilla beans nestled with fine sugar in a closed jar. In a few weeks, you'll have strongly flavored and aromatic vanilla sugar.*

MAKES 1 (9- TO 10-INCH/ 23- TO 25-CM) CAKE

FOR THE DOUGH
· 2 ½ cups plus 2 tablespoons (330 g) all-purpose flour, plus more for dusting
· 1 ¼ cups plus 2 tablespoons (130 g) confectioners' sugar
· ½ cup plus 2 tablespoons (150 g) unsalted butter, cubed
· 1 egg and 5 egg yolks
· 1 tablespoon coarse sea salt

FOR THE FILLING
· 5 medium apples, cored and cut into eighths
· 1 ¼ cups (200 g) raisins
· 2 teaspoons ground cinnamon

FOR THE ALMOND MIXTURE
· ¾ cup (1 ½ sticks/165 g) unsalted butter, melted
· 2 ⅓ cups (330 g) almond flour
· ¾ cup plus 1 tablespoon (165 g) granulated sugar
· ¼ cup (50 g) vanilla sugar (see Tip)
· 4 eggs
· 3 ½ ounces (100 ml) dark rum

FOR THE CRUMBLE
· 6 tablespoons (¾ stick/85 g) unsalted butter, melted
· 6 tablespoons (80 g) granulated sugar
· ⅔ cup (85 g) all-purpose flour
· ¾ cup (85 g) almond flour
· 1 tablespoon coarse sea salt

WHAT YOU NEED
· 9- to 10-inch (23- to 25-cm) springform pan
· Heat shield
· Standard grid
· Pizza stone

TEMPERATURE
· 355°F (180°C)

Technique: baking pizza

Pizza at Low Temperature

This pizza recipe is suited for a temperature below 570°F (300°C). This gives it a softer, more breadlike crust in comparison with the thin-crusted pizza featured on page 88.

Because of the generous amount of yeast used, you don't have to let the dough rise before putting it in the kamado. The leavening happens while you are baking it.

· Make the dough: In a stand mixer fitted with a dough hook, combine all the dough ingredients until you get a cohesive mass. Shape the dough into a ball with your hands, wrap it in plastic wrap, and refrigerate it for 30 minutes.
· Make the tomato sauce: Heat the oil in a skillet over medium heat and sauté the onion, celery, thyme, and coriander. Add the tomatoes and honey. Let them simmer for about 15 minutes. Puree the sauce with an immersion blender, then reduce it over low heat until thick. Season it with a pinch of salt and pepper to taste and then add the basil. Allow the sauce to cool for about 10 minutes before using it on the pizza.
· Fire up the kamado with the heat shield, grid, and pizza stone in place to 525°F (275°C).
· Lightly dust a work surface with flour. Divide the dough into three

equal portions and use a rolling pin to make round disks about ¼ inch (6 mm) thick, making sure that the diameter is smaller than that of the pizza stone.
· Dust the pizza peel with flour and arrange one dough disk on it.
· Spread the dough surface with a generous amount of the sauce. Leave a margin of ¾ inch (2 cm) around the edge and brush the edge with oil. Arrange the asparagus, onion, and mushrooms over the pizza and season with salt and pepper. Scatter the cheese on top.
· Sprinkle the pizza stone with 1 tablespoon of the cornmeal. Slide the pizza gently onto the pizza stone and close the dome.
· After 4 minutes open the kamado and rotate the pizza 90 degrees. Peek under the dough to see whether it's burning.
· Take the pizza off the stone when the bottom is brown, the crust risen, and the cheese bubbly. This will take a total of 5 to 8 minutes.
· Repeat the process with the remaining dough and toppings.

TIP *Of course you can endlessly vary your pizza toppings. We like to keep this pizza recipe completely vegetarian and then add a pronounced flavor with cheeses like Gorgonzola, blue Stilton, or Pecorino.*

MAKES 3 PIZZAS

FOR THE DOUGH
· 3 ⅓ cups (435 g) all-purpose flour, plus more for dusting
· About ¾ cup (180 ml) warm water (110 to 115°F/43 to 46°C)
· ¼ cup (60 ml) white wine
· 1 ounce fresh yeast or 1 tablespoon active dry yeast
· 1 tablespoon honey
· 2 teaspoons sea salt
· 1 tablespoon olive oil classico

FOR THE TOMATO SAUCE
· 1 tablespoon olive oil
· 1 white onion, coarsely chopped
· 1 celery stalk, coarsely chopped
· 3 sprigs fresh thyme, leaves stripped
· 1 tablespoon coriander seeds
· 6 Roma tomatoes, chopped
· 2 tablespoons honey
· Fine sea salt
· Freshly ground black pepper
· 15 fresh basil leaves, finely chopped

FOR THE TOPPINGS
· Olive oil, for brushing
· 10 stalks green asparagus, cut into ¾-inch (2-cm) pieces
· 1 red onion, cut into half-moons
· 3 ½ ounces (100 g) wild mushrooms, sliced
· Sea salt
· Freshly ground black pepper
· 1 ¾ cups (200 g) grated Parmesan or other aged cheese
· 3 tablespoons coarse cornmeal

WHAT YOU NEED
· Immersion blender
· Heat shield
· Standard grid
· Pizza stone and peel

TEMPERATURE
· 525°F (275°C)

Grilled Wild Boar Rib Rack with a Coffee-Chestnut Sauce

For wild boar, the back leg is the prime cut, although other delicious cuts include pork chops and ribs. We choose a rib roast, also called a rack, for this recipe. The taste is distinctly wild, which calls for a robustly flavored sauce.

· Make the sauce: Melt the butter in a skillet over medium heat and sauté the chestnuts until they brown, about 5 minutes. Add the mushrooms; sauté them until they release their liquid and are tender, about 3 minutes. Stir in the flour and cook, stirring, until there is no trace of white left, about 1 minute. Deglaze the pan with the beer, bring to a simmer, and simmer for 2 minutes. Pour in 2½ cups (600 ml) of the broth.

· Let the sauce gently simmer for about 10 minutes. Season it with salt and pepper to taste.

· Stir the cognac and coffee into the sauce and take off the heat.

· Prepare the meat: Rub the racks with salt and pepper.

· Fire up the kamado with the cast-iron grid to about 390°F (200°C). Create a broad grilling surface out of three hot spots.

· Cooking time depends on the size and weight of the pork cuts; expect it to take 30 to 40 minutes.

· Place the racks on the grid convex-side down. Grill for 2 minutes, then turn 90 degrees for 2 minutes, creating a crosshatch pattern. Repeat on the bone side, cooking for 3 minutes, then 4 minutes.

· Take the meat out of the kamado and install the heat shield and the drip pan. Replace the grid and put the meat back on it. Reduce the temperature over 10 minutes by squeezing off the air supply in both the top and bottom vents.

· Close the dome and cook until the internal temperature of the racks reaches a safe 155°F (68°C), 30 to 40 minutes.

· Put the sauce back over low heat to rewarm, adding more broth if it's too thick.

· Remove the racks from the grill and let them rest for 5 minutes, then divide the boar into cutlets. Season with salt and pepper. If the meat is still a little too pink, you can put it back on the grill. Serve the cutlets with the sauce.

TIP *You can serve roasted potatoes and beets as a side dish (see recipe, page 106).*

SERVES 4 TO 6

FOR THE SAUCE
- 1 tablespoon butter
- 7 ounces (200 g) roasted chestnuts, sliced
- 7 ounces (200 g) wild mushrooms, such as chanterelles or *pied de mouton*
- 1 tablespoon all-purpose flour
- About ¾ cup (180 ml) dark beer
- 2 ½ to 3 cups (600 to 720 ml) game or chicken broth
- Coarse sea salt
- Freshly ground black pepper
- Splash of cognac
- Shot of coffee

FOR THE MEAT
- 2 (14- to 20-ounce/400- to 600-g) racks wild boar, pan ready
- Coarse sea salt
- Freshly ground black pepper

WHAT YOU NEED
- Cast-iron grid
- Heat shield
- Drip pan
- Food thermometer

TEMPERATURE
- 280 to 390°F (140 to 200°C)

Moroccan-Style Leg of Lamb

You can find locally sourced lamb chops at most farmers' markets, but your butcher may also sell them at a reasonable price. Ask for a whole leg of lamb. We source the lamb meat we serve at our restaurant, Pure Passie, from a local flock of *Shoonebeker Heideschapen* (a Dutch sheep breed, traditionally used for grazing heather). During their lives, these sheep are used for the sustainable management of a nature reserve in the Westland (an agricultural area near The Hague). They live strictly off the land and don't receive any additional food. This is why their meat has an exceptionally mild flavor.

· Make the wet rub: Crush the cumin, coriander, and salt together in a mortar. Add the chile peppers, garlic, lemon zest, black pepper, and mint. Crush them to a coarse paste. Stir in the oil and lemon juice. Thoroughly coat the lamb with the wet rub. Cover and refrigerate it to marinate, preferably for 12 hours.
· Fire up the kamado with the heat shield, the standard grid, and drip pan with a layer of water to 212°F (100°C).

· Place the leg of lamb on the grid and close the lid. Cook it until the meat reaches an internal temperature of 125°F (52°C), 3 to 3½ hours.
· Remove the meat from the grid and wrap it in aluminum foil. Take out the standard grid and the heat shield. Put back the grid and then stoke up the kamado to 390°F (200°C).
· Unwrap and grill the leg of lamb under a closed lid for about 10 minutes, until it has a golden crust all around. This grilling will raise the internal temperature another 5 degrees to medium or medium-well done.
· Remove the lamb to a cutting board to rest for a few minutes.
· Cut the leg into four thick slices by cutting through the bone. Subsequently cut these slices against the grain.

TIP *This leg of lamb tastes wonderful with an avocado salad.*

SERVES 6 TO 8

FOR THE WET RUB
· 2 tablespoons cumin seeds
· 3 tablespoons coriander seeds
· 2 tablespoons coarse sea salt
· 2 jalapeño or serrano peppers, seeded and minced
· 7 cloves garlic, minced
· Zest and juice of 2 lemons
· 2 tablespoons freshly ground black pepper
· 4 sprigs fresh mint, leaves stripped
· 6 tablespoons (90 ml) olive oil

FOR THE MEAT
· 5 ½ pounds (2.5 kg) leg of lamb

WHAT YOU NEED
· Heat shield
· Standard grid
· Drip pan
· Food thermometer

TEMPERATURE
· 212 to 390°F (100 to 200°C)

Wild Rabbit Stew

During hunting season, wild rabbits can be bought locally. In the summer, we tend to work with farmed rabbit instead. Ask your butcher to cut up the rabbit into six parts.

· Fire up the kamado with the cast-iron grid to 390°F (200°C). Light up a wide triangle of hot spots.

· Salt the rabbit parts first. Grill the rabbit cuts for a few minutes until golden brown (don't worry about grill marks) and set them aside.

· Place the Dutch oven without the lid on the grid. Add the butter and let it melt. Sauté the onion, leek, and mushrooms until the onion is nicely translucent, about 8 minutes. Close the lid of the kamado between each action.

· Add the carrot, sage, and garlic and sauté them for another minute or two. Stir in the flour and continue cooking for a minute. Deglaze the pan with the beer and use a wooden spatula to scrape up any food sticking to the bottom.

· Place the rabbit cuts in the Dutch oven and pour in the broth until the meat is just about submerged. Add the juniper berries and bay leaves and stir them around a couple of times. Close the lid of the Dutch oven and take it out of the kamado. Place the heat shield on top of the grid and put back the Dutch oven. The temperature of the kamado should be around 265°F (130°C).

· Now stew the rabbit, keeping the kamado lid closed, for at least 45 minutes. Then check whether the rabbit is done. You should be able to easily pull the meat from the bone, but it shouldn't come off by itself yet. Stew it a little longer if needed.

· Remove the Dutch oven to a heatproof trivet. If the gravy is a little too watery, then spoon out a little of the liquid and mix it with the cornstarch. Stir it back into the stew and put it back on the kamado to simmer until thickened. Discard the bay leaves.

· Stir the sour cream into the warm broth, making sure to incorporate it thoroughly; heat through, but do not let the broth boil. Season with salt and pepper to taste and serve.

TIP *In the summer, you can make this dish with farmed rabbit cuts, using dark beer instead of blonde beer. You can also add a few sliced figs to the stew.*

SERVES 4

· Coarse salt
· 4 (1 3/4-pound/800-g) rabbits, or 3 larger rabbits, cleaned and cut into six pieces each
· 1 tablespoon butter
· 1 white onion, coarsely chopped
· 1/2 leek, coarsely chopped
· 7 ounces (200 g) champignon (white button) mushrooms, quartered
· 1 winter carrot, coarsely chopped
· Several fresh sage leaves, sliced
· 2 cloves garlic, minced
· 1 tablespoon flour
· 1 cup (240 ml) high-fermentation blonde beer
· About 2 cups (480 ml) chicken broth
· 3 crushed juniper berries
· 2 bay leaves
· 1 1/2 teaspoons cornstarch (optional)
· 2 tablespoons sour cream
· Freshly ground black pepper

WHAT YOU NEED
· Cast-iron grid
· Dutch oven (at least 5 quarts/ 4.7 L)
· Wooden spatula
· Heat shield

TEMPERATURE
· 265 to 390°F (130 to 200°C)

Duck Breast with Orange and Thyme

In this recipe, you'll encounter every technique that could possibly be applied to preparing meat: grilling, smoking, and searing in a pan. We like to buy big, fat, farmed duck breast, since these can withstand all kinds of temperature changes without the risk of drying out. The intention is to allow the taste of smoke to penetrate the meat and fatty parts. That way you'll get a mild greasy fume during grilling and a nice Maillard reaction in the pan—a harmonious combination of all the techniques. Searing in a pan or on a griddle will brown the meat on the fatty skin side without setting the coals on fire.

· With a small, sharp knife, remove the membranes and tendons from the duck breast. Score the fatty skin in a crosshatch pattern. Place the duck fillets between two layers of orange slices and thyme sprigs and lay them on a baking sheet or in a shallow pan. Apply pressure by placing a container filled with water on top and refrigerate them for 2 hours.

· Fire up the kamado to 265 to 280°F (130 to 140°C) and create one hot spot. Then reconfigure the kamado for smoking at about 200°F (90°C). Place the smoking wood on top of the hot spot and install the heat shield. Wait until the kamado begins to smoke. Fill the drip pan with water and add the orange slices and thyme for added flavor. Place the pan on the heat shield and install the grid.

· Place the duck breasts on the grid, skin-side up. Smoke them for about 20 minutes, until the internal temperature reaches between 122 and 127°F (50 and 52°C).

· Remove the duck breasts and wrap them in aluminum foil. Remove the grid, the drip pan, and the heat shield. Return the grid and place the skillet or griddle on top. Heat up the kamado to 390°F (200°C).

· Grill the duck breasts flesh-side down on the grid until fumes develop. Turn the duck breasts over into the skillet. Fry the skin sides for about 2 minutes to crisp them.

· You can leave the dome open while you're pan-searing the meat to check that the skin doesn't blacken. Using gloves, lift the skillet or griddle out of the kamado and make sure no hot grease splashes over your hands.

· Remove the duck breasts to a cutting board and allow them to rest for a few minutes before you slice them diagonally in thin slices. A good core temperature is 135 to 140°F (58 to 60°C).

SERVES 4 AS A SMALL MAIN COURSE OR 6 AS A STARTER

· 2 (10 1/2-ounce/300-g) farmed duck breasts *(magret de canard)*
· 2 oranges, cut into 1/2-inch (12-mm) slices
· 1 bunch fresh thyme
· Coarse salt
· Freshly ground black pepper

WHAT YOU NEED

· Cherrywood for smoking (1 small chunk or a handful of chips)
· Heat shield
· Drip pan
· Standard grid
· Food thermometer
· Skillet or cast-iron griddle

TEMPERATURE

· 200 to 390°F (90 to 200°C)

TIP *This preparation guarantees a deliciously complex flavor. You can serve the duck breasts with chutney, in which sweet, sour, and spicy flavors blend together. The duck fat that remains in the skillet can be used to fry potatoes, such as the twice-baked potatoes mentioned on page 98.*

Turkey on a Poultry Stand

Turkeys are large birds, native to North and Central America. These days, they are farmed all over the world for their meat. Not all turkeys are created equally, however. We like to work with Label Rouge turkeys. These slow-growing breeds have been selected for their meat quality. They are free to roam in the open air and are butchered relatively late in their lives. The result is soft and tender meat with a slightly darker color than that of a traditional turkey, and a little gamey flavor.

· First check whether the pot fits your refrigerator; if not, find another large container to hold the turkey and brine.

· Make the brine: In a large pot, combine the hot water with the salt and sugar so that the salt and sugar dissolve. Add the cold water, and allow the liquid to cool. Squeeze juice from the lemons into the brine and then add the slices and tarragon.

· Place the turkey in the pot with the brine. Make sure the turkey is completely submerged. If this isn't the case, make some extra brine. Cover the pot with a lid, aluminum foil, or plastic wrap, then refrigerate it for at least 24 hours.

· Fire up the kamado with the heat shield to 300°F (150°C).

· Remove the turkey from the brine and place it on the stand. If the legs haven't been tied together, do this yourself with some butcher's twine. Place the bird, stand and all, in the roasting tray. Then put the tray on the heat shield and close the dome.

· Cook the turkey for 2½ to 3 hours, until the thigh has reached an internal temperature of 160°F (70°C). If desired, you can allow the temperature under the dome to go up to 355°F (180°C) for the last half-hour to give the turkey skin an even darker golden brown color.

· Remove the turkey and stand to a cutting board. Let it cool for at least 10 minutes before removing it from the stand and carving the meat.

TIP *Roasted turkey is delicious with cranberry compote or classic Madeira gravy.*

SERVES 6

FOR THE BRINE
· 2 cups (480 ml) hot water
· 10 ½ ounces (300 g) sea salt
· 1 cup (200 g) packed light brown sugar
· 5 quarts (4.7 L) cold water
· 4 lemons, cut into wedges
· 10 sprigs fresh tarragon, coarsely chopped

FOR THE MEAT
· 1 (6 ½-pound/3-kg) turkey

WHAT YOU NEED
· Large pot
· Turkey stand
· Heat shield
· Butcher's twine (if necessary)
· Large drip pan or roasting tray
· Food thermometer

TEMPERATURE
· 300 to 355°F (150 to 180°C)

Smoked Rillettes with Crispy Ears

Our friend Peter Bootsma, who gave us this recipe, calls it a "slacker's dish," meaning that he makes this whenever he doesn't have anything else to do. This is the type of dish that you prepare mostly a day—or several days—in advance. You only need to perform a few tasks near the kamado over the span of an entire day. The rest is merely a matter of being daring.

· First thoroughly clean the head. If necessary, you can use a scrub brush to remove any dirt. Then make sure the pieces of your pig's head actually fit into your pan.
· Fire up the kamado with a single hot spot to 265°F (130°C). Place the wood on top of the charcoal. Configure the kamado for indirect smoking and place the heat shield and drip pan.

· Put the pig's head halves on the grid, cut-sides facing down. Let them smoke and slow-cook for 5 hours at a temperature of 225°F (110°C).
· Remove the pig's head halves from the grill and set them aside on a baking sheet. Take out the heat shield and the grid, then return just the grid. The temperature in the kamado should go up to about 320°F (160°C).
· Fill up the Dutch oven with the carrot, leek, onion, and the pig's head halves. Add the broth until the halves are submerged. Place the pot on the grill. Close the kamado lid and let the pot simmer for 4 to 5 hours, until the skin begins to come loose. If the broth is cooking too rapidly, put back the heat shield in between the grid and the pan.

SERVES 4 TO 6 AS A STARTER OR SNACK

FOR THE RILLETTES
· 1 pig's head, cut in half and rinsed
· 1/2 winter carrot, coarsely chopped
· 1 leek, thickly sliced into rings
· 1 white onion, quartered
· 3 quarts (2.8 L) chicken broth
· Coarse sea salt

WHAT YOU NEED
· 1 chunk hickory smoking wood
· Heat shield
· Drip pan
· Standard grid
· Dutch oven or large pan of at least 5 quarts (4.7 L)

(CONTINUED ON PAGE 152)

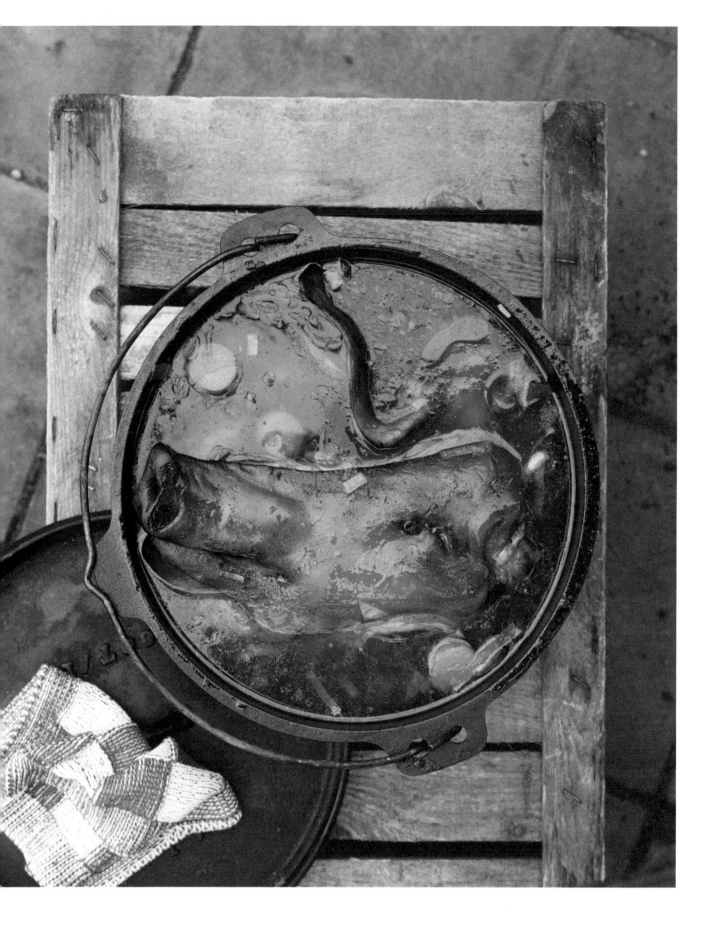

(CONTINUED FROM PAGE 150)

· Make the dressing: In a bowl, mix together the shallot, mustard, vinegar, and chives. Whisk while pouring in the oil until you get an opaque, homogenous dressing. Season it with some salt and pepper to taste.

· Take out the pig's head pieces from the broth. If you strain the broth, you can later use it for a soup.

· Remove the skin from the entire head. Cut off the ears. Skin the ears until you are left with just the white cartilage. Set this cartilage aside.

· Pull the meat (especially the cheeks) and the fat from the bones. Season the meat with the dressing. Put the meat in a jar and the ears in a separate container, and refrigerate everything for at least one day.

· Fire up the kamado with the standard grid to 390°F (200°C). Dab dry the ears with a paper towel and sprinkle them with salt. Slice each ear into four strips. Grill the pig's ear strips until they are crisp, 6 to 8 minutes. This is easier said than done and noncrispy parts can become rather tough.

· Serve the rillettes cold on toast with cornichons or pickled onions. Sprinkle with an extra teaspoon of dressing and chives. Serve the crispy ears as a side dish.

TIP *Using the rillettes, crispy ears, and dressing, you can also make a nice pig's head salad.*

FOR THE DRESSING

· 1/2 shallot, minced
· 1 teaspoon whole-grain mustard
· 1 tablespoon white wine vinegar
· 1 tablespoon finely chopped fresh chives
· 2 tablespoons olive oil
· Coarse salt
· Freshly ground black pepper

FOR SERVING

· Toast
· Cornichons or pickled onions
· 1 tablespoon finely chopped fresh chives

TEMPERATURE

· 225 to 390°F (110 to 200°C)

SOURCES

Books:

Bottéro, Jean. *The Oldest Cuisine in the World: Cooking in Mesopotamia.* Chicago: University of Chicago Press, 2004.

Curtis, Robert I. *Ancient Food Technology.* Leiden/Boston: Brill, 2001.

Fisher, Ed. *Hatching the Big Green Egg.* New Word City, Inc., 2011.

Homma, Gaku. *The Folk Art of Japanese Country Cooking: A Traditional Diet for Today's World.* Berkeley, CA: North Atlantic Books; Denver, CO: Domo Productions, 1991.

Ishige, Naomichi. *The History and Culture of Japanese Food.* London/ New York: Kegan Paul, 2001.

Kazerouni, N., R. Sinha, Che-Han Hsu, A. Greenberg, N. Rothman. "Analysis of 200 food items for benzo[a]pyrene and estimation of its intake in an epidemiological study." *Food and Chemical Toxicology* 39, 2001.

Klosse, Peter, et al. *Het proefboek: The essentie van smaak [The Essence of Taste].* Baarn: Tirion, 2003.

McGee, Harold. *On Food and Cooking: The Science and Lore of the Kitchen.* New York: Scribner, 2004.

Ruhlman, Michael, and Brian Polcyn. *Charcuterie: The Craft of Salting, Smoking, and Curing.* New York: W.W. Norton, 2005.

Symons, Michael. *A History of Cooks and Cooking.* Champaign, IL: University of Illinois Press, 2000.

Tannahill, Reay. *Food in History, rev. ed.* New York: Broadway Books, 1995.

Websites:

Amazing Ribs
amazingribs.com
Craig "Meathead" Goldwyn

Genuine Ideas
genuineideas.com
Dr. Greg Blonder

Naked Whiz
nakedwhiz.com

ACKNOWLEDGMENTS

Jeroen:

I most of all want to thank Peter Bootsma for the first steps, the pig snout, and all of his emotional support. I would also like to thank:

My sounding board, **Gerard den Bakker**, who put me on the right path and introduced me to Joe. **Eddie Rahakbauw**, for the first fire pit in the province of Groningen. **Ralp de Kok**, who, just like me, taught himself to cook on the kamado and who arrived at the same result via a completely different method. **Ton van Veen**, for the discussion in the car back and forth to Naples. **Dirk**, for the sand. **Dr. Greg Blonder**, for getting the science right. **Brian Moriarty** (Swampbrdr), for printing out important historical information in 2001 and for taking the efforts to send it across the Atlantic in 2013. **My father**, for teaching me the benefits of stainless steel, cast iron, and other nonsense. And last, but not least, **my mother** and **Dick**, for the garden and all their support.

Leo:

The inspiration for this book all started at my restaurant, Pure Passie, in 's-Gravenzande, Netherlands. That's where I first started using the kamado a few years ago.

I noticed how versatile the kamado was and began to get excited. I used the kamado a lot and noted this on our menu. Many of our guests were raving about the grill and the dishes we prepared with it; however, there was much confusion about using the kamado, so I started giving workshops. Eventually I began writing this book, which allows everyone to enjoy using the kamado. So, dear Pure Passie guests—thanks!

I would like to thank **Jan van Bronswijk**, for perfecting the bread recipes.

I would also like to thank all my **friends and family** for their support via Twitter and Facebook.

GLOSSARY

Band – The steel rings that bind the dome and the base to the hinges. The upper ring has a handle.

Back draft – If there is low pressure in a hot kamado, there can be a sudden influx of oxygen when the dome is opened. The kamado may then briefly produce a blue, hot flame.

Base – The lower part of the kamado. The fire box stands on the bottom of the base.

Bottom vent – The metal slide at the base of the kamado. Used for regulating the airflow at the bottom.

Brine – A saltwater bath used for soaking a piece of meat or an entire bird for a few hours or a full day, allowing the salt to permeate the meat. In the hot kamado, this salt helps the meat to retain its moisture so it won't dry out as quickly. Brines are also used to preserve food. To add flavors to the meat, you can add herbs, spices, and sugar to the brine.

Browning reactions – This is used to describe all chemical reactions that contribute to the browning process of an ingredient, like Maillard and caramelization.

Caramelization – A complex chemical reaction in which heat browns sugar and changes its taste and color.

Cast iron – A cast, porous metal with unique heat characteristics. Grids, pans, and accessories are made from it. When seasoning cast iron, it absorbs fat and gets a natural nonstick coating.

Caveman style – All preparations in which the main ingredient is placed directly on the charcoal.

Ceramic – A hard, crystalline material made from baked clay, sometimes glazed.

Chips – Small pieces of wood for smoking.

Chunk – A piece of wood for smoking.

Convection – Hot air circulation or airflow.

ConvEGGtor (plate setter) – The ceramic heat shield from the Big Green Egg brand. Because it has three legs, there's no need for a rack or grid to put it on.

Cuisson – (French) The degree to which food is cooked. Doneness.

Daisy wheel – A dual-function metal top for the dome vent. The larger part that regulates oxygen supply can be fine-tuned by adjusting the smaller openings.

Dome – The upper part of the kamado, the lid.

D-Plates – The two-piece heat shield of the Primo brand.

Dutch oven – A cast-iron pot with a flat bottom, used for cooking over open fire and on the grill. The open-fire version often has legs that aren't very suited for use in a kamado. Also used as a bread oven.

Enamel – A hard, glossy substance used to protect metal grids and accessories.

False air – Oxygen unintentionally flowing toward the charcoal through a leak between the dome and the base of the kamado. This can be caused by a damaged or wrongly assembled felt gasket or a badly aligned lid.

Fire box – The ceramic part inside the base of the kamado with small holes in the bottom. Used for holding the charcoal.

Fire ring – The ring-shaped segment that can be placed on top of the fire box to raise the grid. With some brands, box and ring are integrated into one ceramic part.

Fire starter – A piece of pressed sawdust drenched in paraffin (petroleum wax).

Flare-up – The flare-up of grease when you open the kamado's dome.

Food thermometer – A thermometer with a probe that you stick into your ingredient.

Fume – Smoke from incompletely combusted fats (and proteins).

Gasket – The sealing and dampening gasket in between the dome and the base of the kamado. Made from felt, Nomex, or some other heat-resistant material.

Glaze – A tough mineral outer layer that's baked in with most ceramic kamados. Due to the difference in expansion with the kamado base material, it can show a visible layer of cracking.

Glow – The radiance of burning charcoal.

Grid lifter – An accessory to lift the grid from the kamado. Exists in two versions: with a cross, and more like tongs.

Grill – Verb: grill. Noun: grid. In American English, "grill" typically refers to the entire apparatus.

Grill plank – A wooden board on top of which you can cook and smoke an ingredient in the grill.

Heat shield – A ceramic or metal

shield that turns a grill into an indirect grill or oven.

Hinge – The metal system connecting the dome and the base of a kamado. Often fitted with one or more spring coils to ease the opening and closing of the heavy lid.

Hot spot – A glow spot in the charcoal mass.

Kamado – In Japan: oven, fireplace, kitchen, furnace, place where rice is cooked and steamed. Outside of Japan: ceramic grill.

Maillard reaction – A complex chemical reaction in which proteins and sugars acquire a brown crust due to the heating process.

Mesh – A little grate shielding the opening of the bottom vent that some brands include to prevent hot ash from falling out of the kamado.

Mushikamado – A Japanese rice cooker. During the 1960s, American entrepreneurs retrofitted the device with a grid, turning the kamado into a ceramic barbecue grill.

Nomex – Heat-resistant fabric used in the protective clothing of firemen and race car drivers. Also used as gasket material in kamados.

Patina – A thin layer of carbon deposit, usually on the inside of the dome. If you don't clean the kamado often enough or when the felt gasket leaks, it can also appear on the outside.

Pellets – Pressed sawdust in the shape of rabbit food; used for smoking.

Pizza stone – A ceramic plate on which you can bake bread, desserts, and pizza. Can sometimes double as a heat shield.

Poker / Ash tool – A long flat metal rod with a 90-degree angle at the end. Universal tool for stirring and moving charcoal and for removing ash.

Rare – Cooked red meat, still bloody.

Rosé – Meat that is semi-tender, but not cooked all the way through; medium or à point.

Rub – A dry or wet spice-and-herb mix, used for marinating. Usually it stays on during cooking. It's also used to induce flavor in the crust shortly before cooking. A dry rub generally consists of spices with salt, sugar, garlic powder, paprika, and chili flakes. When applied a few hours in advance, a dry rub can function as a dry brine. A wet rub is usually made of fresh herbs and chili peppers. These can fall off during cooking.

Side tables – Little platforms attached to both sides of the kamado (usually to the bottom ring of the belt, but sometimes to the rack). Not meant to hold heavy loads.

Skillet – A cast-iron frying pan with a short handle. Suitable for use on open fire and in the grill.

Stainless steel – A steel alloy treated against corrosion and rust.

Tandoor (*tandyr, tannur, tanur*) – A traditional ceramic vessel that has been used as a bread oven for five thousand years throughout large parts of Asia and the Middle East.

Top vent regulator – A rotatable disk on top of the dome of the kamado. Used for regulating the airflow on top. Some brands call it a "daisy wheel."

Well-done – Thoroughly cooked meat or *bien cuit*.

Wood smoke – The incomplete combustion of wood, which generates hundreds of volatiles.

Yan steamer – A ceramic Chinese rice cooker from the Qin dynasty. This vessel consists of three parts: a fire box, a water pan, and a perforated pot to hold the uncooked rice.

INDEX

RECIPES

Originally published in 2014 by
Fontaine Uitgevers BV, Hilversum
www.fontaineuitgevers.nl

DESIGN durk.com
PHOTOGRAPHY Saskia van Osnabrugge
STYLING Annemieke Paarlberg
ILLUSTRATIONS Studio Michels, Trudy Michels
CULINARY EDITOR Inge van der Helm
EDITOR Christine Bosch

Published in 2015 by Stewart, Tabori & Chang
An imprint of ABRAMS

EDITORS Holly Dolce and Sarah Massey
PRODUCTION MANAGER Katie Gaffney
TRANSLATED FROM DUTCH BY Marleen Reimer & Victor Verbeek

Library of Congress Control Number:
2014948545

ISBN: 978-1-61769-158-4

The text of this book was composed in Forza and Mercury.

Printed and bound in the United States

10 9 8 7 6 5 4 3 2 1

Stewart, Tabori & Chang books are available at special discounts when purchased in quantity for premiums and promotions as well as fundraising or educational use. Special editions can also be created to specification. For details, contact specialsales@abramsbooks.com or the address below.

115 West 18th Street
New York, NY 10011
www.abramsbooks.com